Mack Munro's

Driving Results Masterclass

The Art of Being a Great Boss

Illustrated and Facilitated by
Mack Munro

BOSSBUILDERS

©2020 Mack Munro. All rights reserved   *(Version 5 – June 2023)*

Get downloadable versions of many of the tools in this course at:
www.TheBossBuilders.com/helps

Session 1

Introduction and Orientation

Welcome to The Art of Being a Great Boss! Over the next 12 sessions we'll learn practical tips and techniques that will help you excel in your role as The Boss and get your direct reports to be more motivated and productive. This first session is an orientation to the program as well as a way to introduce yourself to your cohort.

Introduction

The Art of Being a Great Boss Masterclass gives clear direction, tools, and techniques to become a more effective supervisor. Each of the 13 sessions includes practical applications designed to give you tools that can be used immediately.

Session 1: Introduction and Orientation

- Welcome to the program and to the participants. Setting learning goals and doing a quick assessment of our skills.

Session 2: Embracing Your Role as The Boss

- What we bring to the role and what's expected of us.

Session 3: Building Relationships for Results Part 1

- Effective Communication.

Session 4: Building Relationships for Results Part 2

- Our default behavior style and how to maximize it.

Session 5: Building Relationships for Results Part 3

- Dealing with conflict and difficult people.

Session 6: Driving Results Part 1

- How to be an effective manager of performance.

Session 7: Driving Results Part 2

- Feedback and coaching techniques.

Session 8: Driving Results Part 3

- Delegation skills. Evaluating team performance. Goal setting.

Session 9: Engaging Employees

- How to create a culture of motivation and engagement.

Session 10: Tools and Their Uses Part 1

- Problem-solving tools and when to use them.

Session 11: Tools and Their Uses Part 2

- Process improvement and decision-making tools and when to use them.

Session 12: Your Power and Influence

- How to identify and leverage your sources of power and influence.

Session 13: Navigating Organizational Politics

- How to use your power and influence to help you and your team win every time.

DAILY TO-DO LIST

- [ ] BUILD _____.
- [ ] DO WHAT YOU _____ YOU WILL DO.
- [ ] DEVELOP _____ CLASS EMPLOYEES.
- [ ] TREAT EMPLOYEES _____.
- [ ] ADDRESS POOR PERFORMANCE _____.
- [ ] ASK BETTER _____.
- [ ] LISTEN MORE. ASSUME LESS _____.
- [ ] _____ ONLY WHEN NECESSARY.
- [ ] CREATE A CULTURE WHERE PEOPLE WOULD WORK FOR _____.
- [ ] SEPARATE WORK FROM LIFE. THERE IS NO _____.
- [ ] _____ SOMETHING NEW TODAY.

©MACE

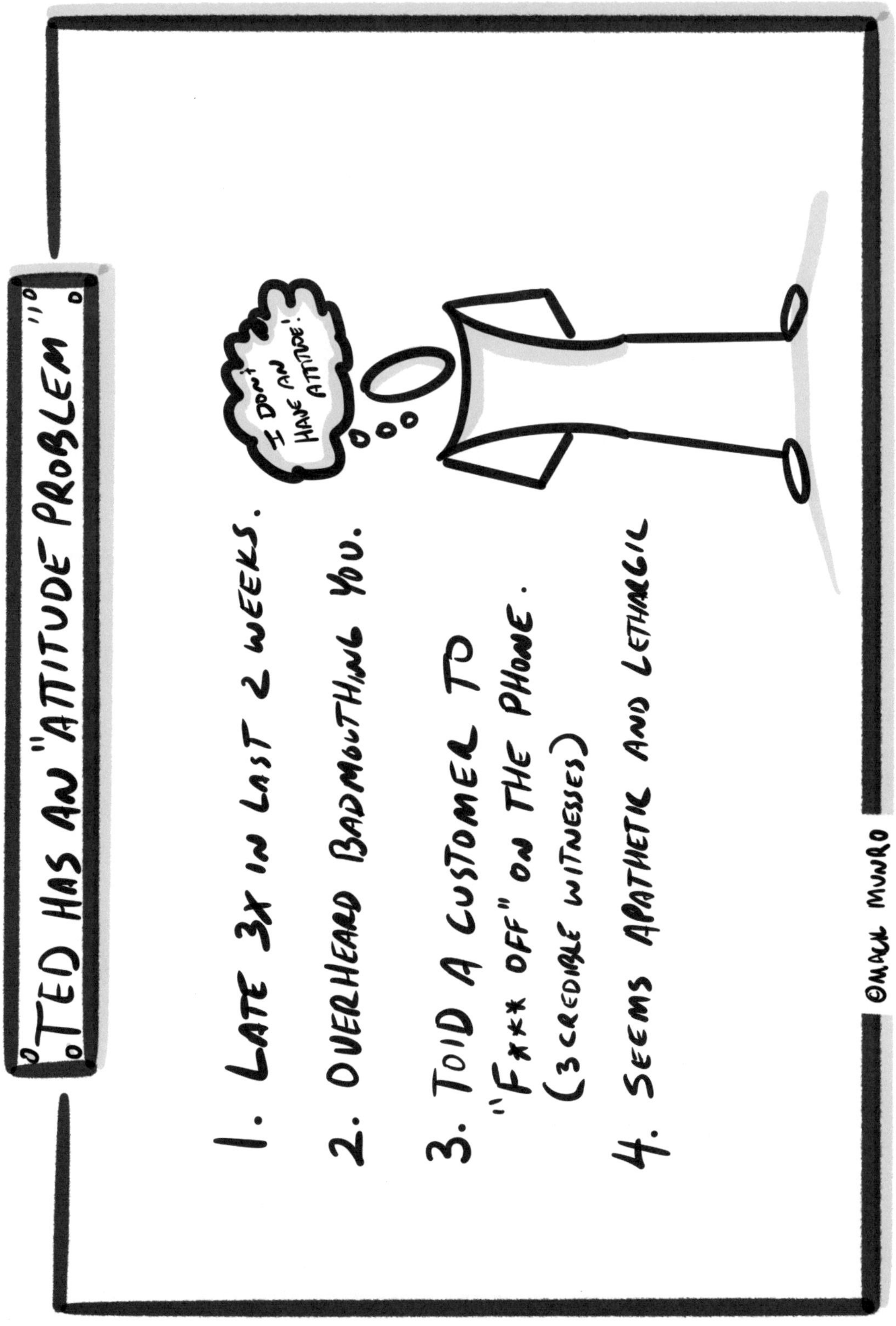
"TED HAS AN "ATTITUDE" PROBLEM"
1. LATE 3X IN LAST 2 WEEKS.
2. OVERHEARD BADMOUTHING YOU.
3. TOLD A CUSTOMER TO "F*** OFF" ON THE PHONE. (3 CREDIBLE WITNESSES)
4. SEEMS APATHETIC AND LETHARGIC
I DON'T HAVE AN ATTITUDE!
©MACK MUNRO

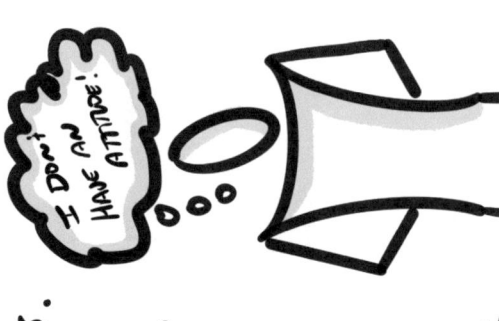

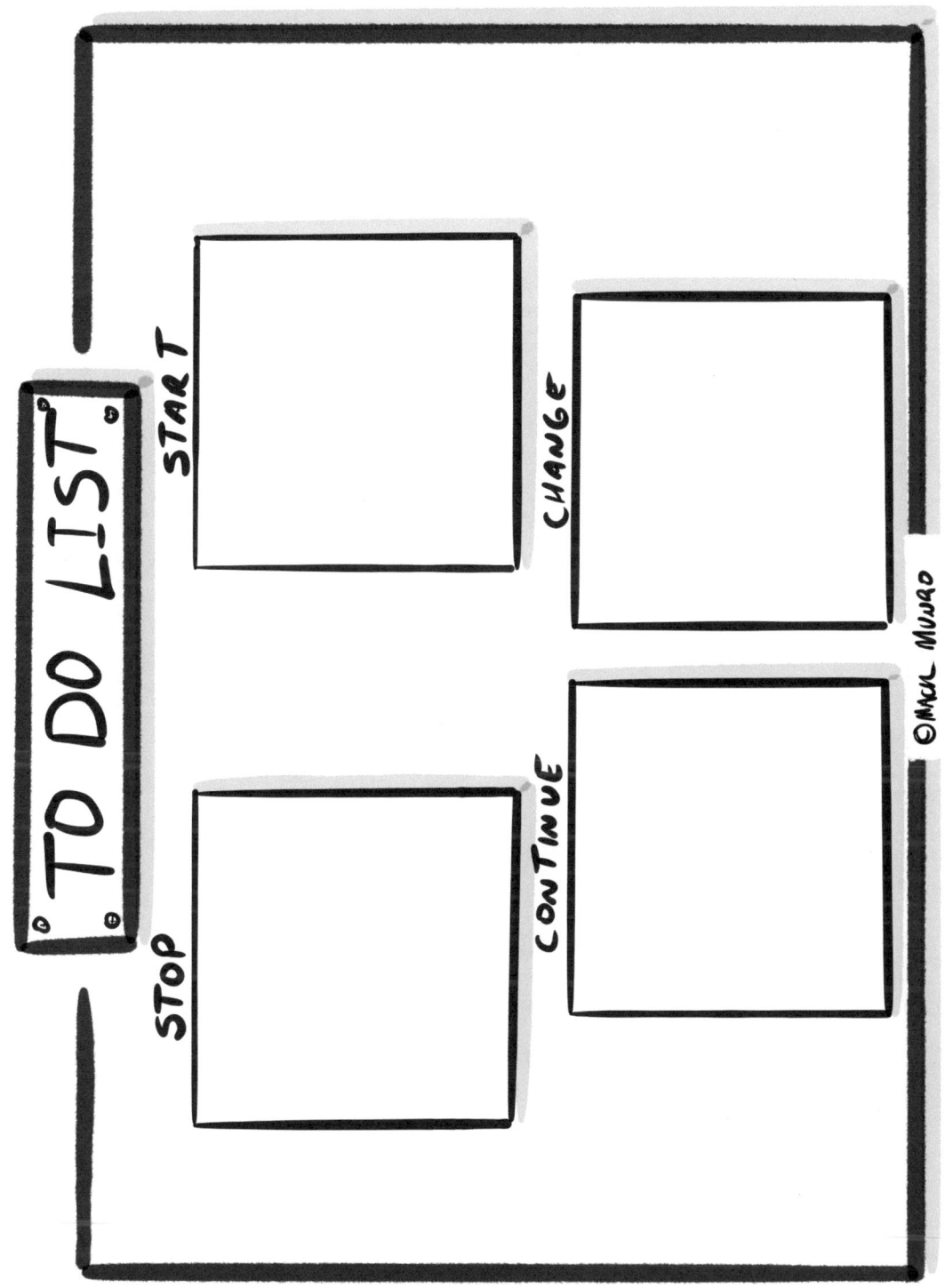

Notes

Session 2

Embracing Your Role as The Boss

The role of a manager is challenging considering the numerous changes you'll face. To be successful, you need to balance the needs of the people against the needs of the organization. To do this requires new skills.

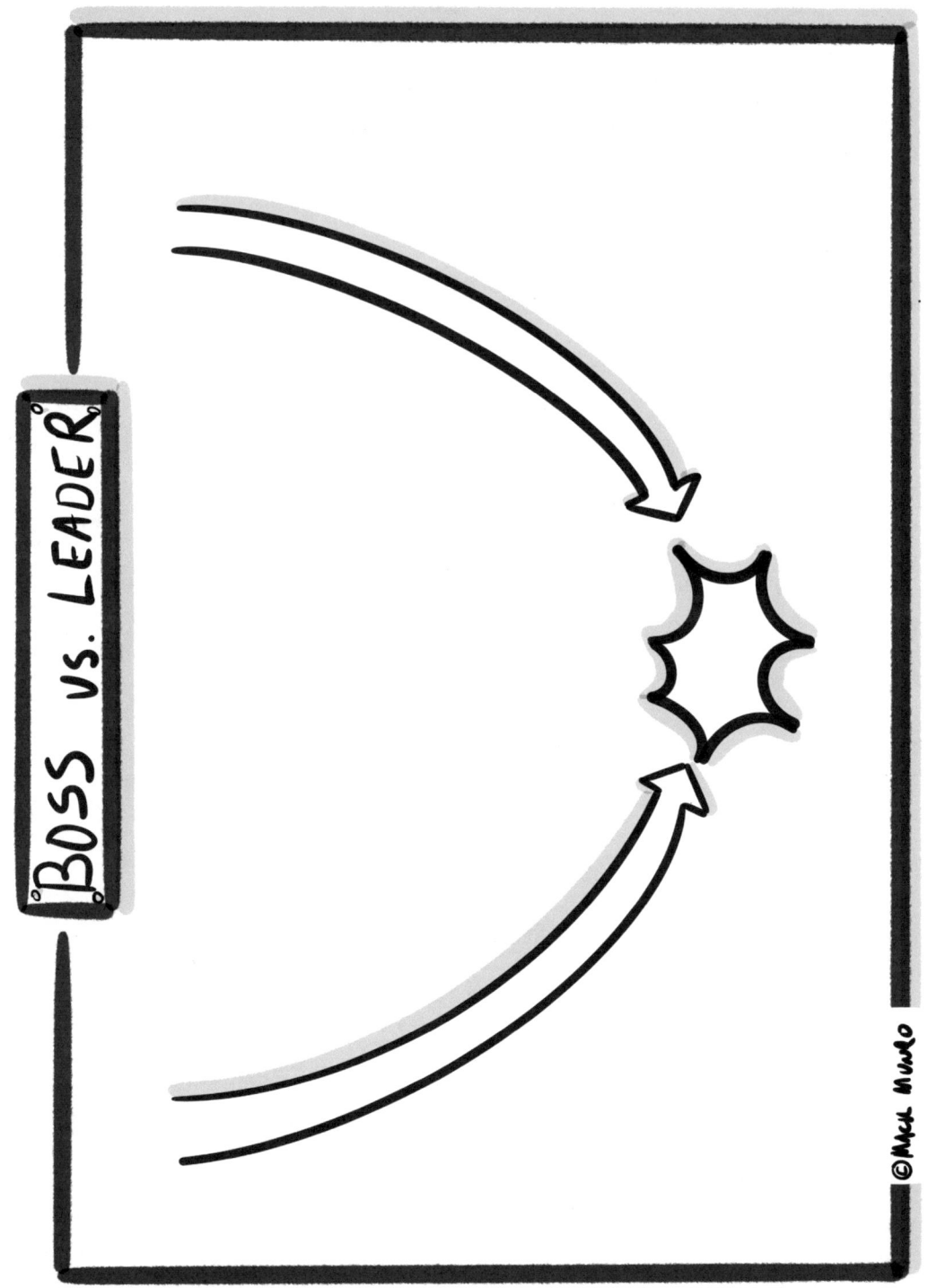

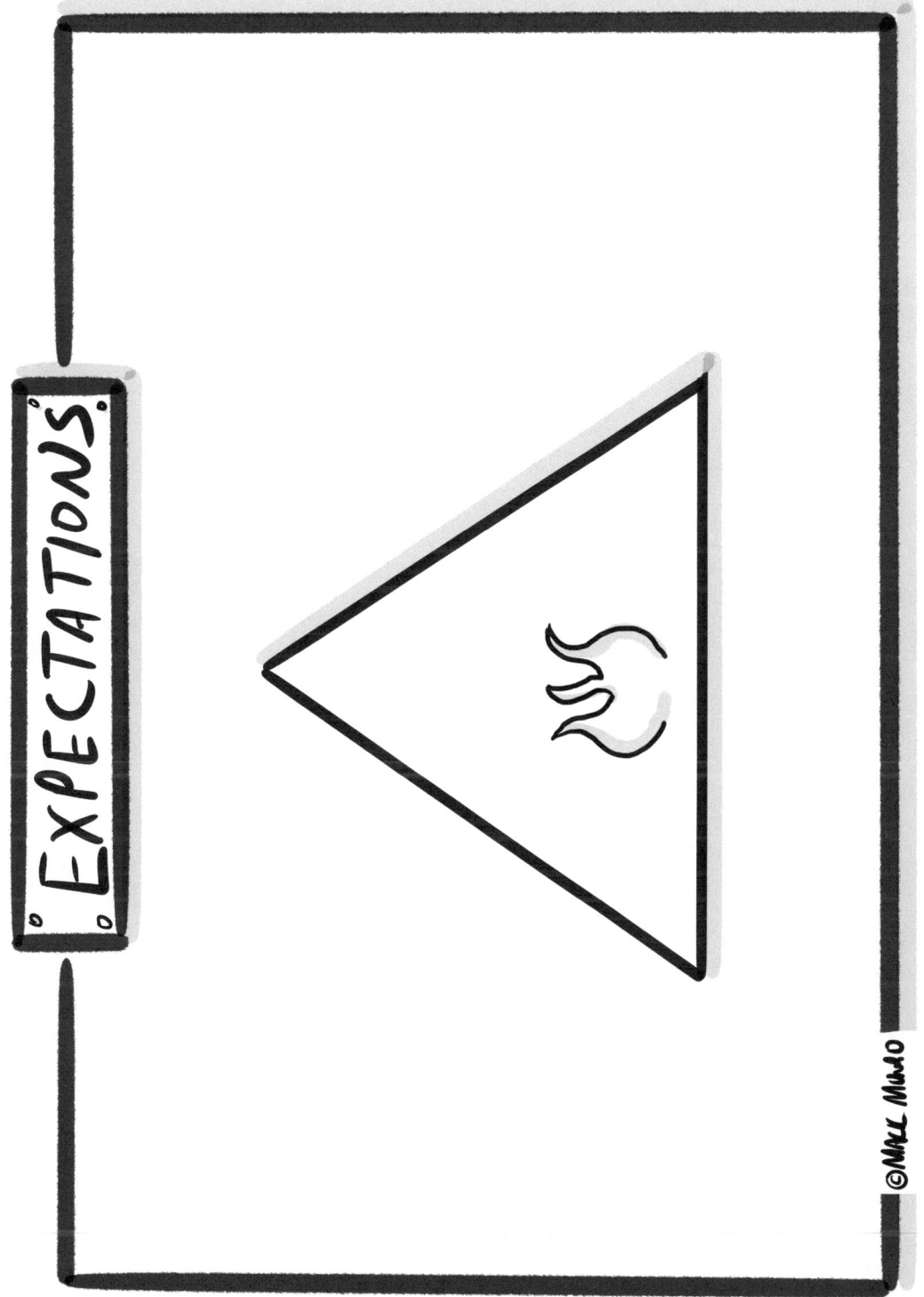

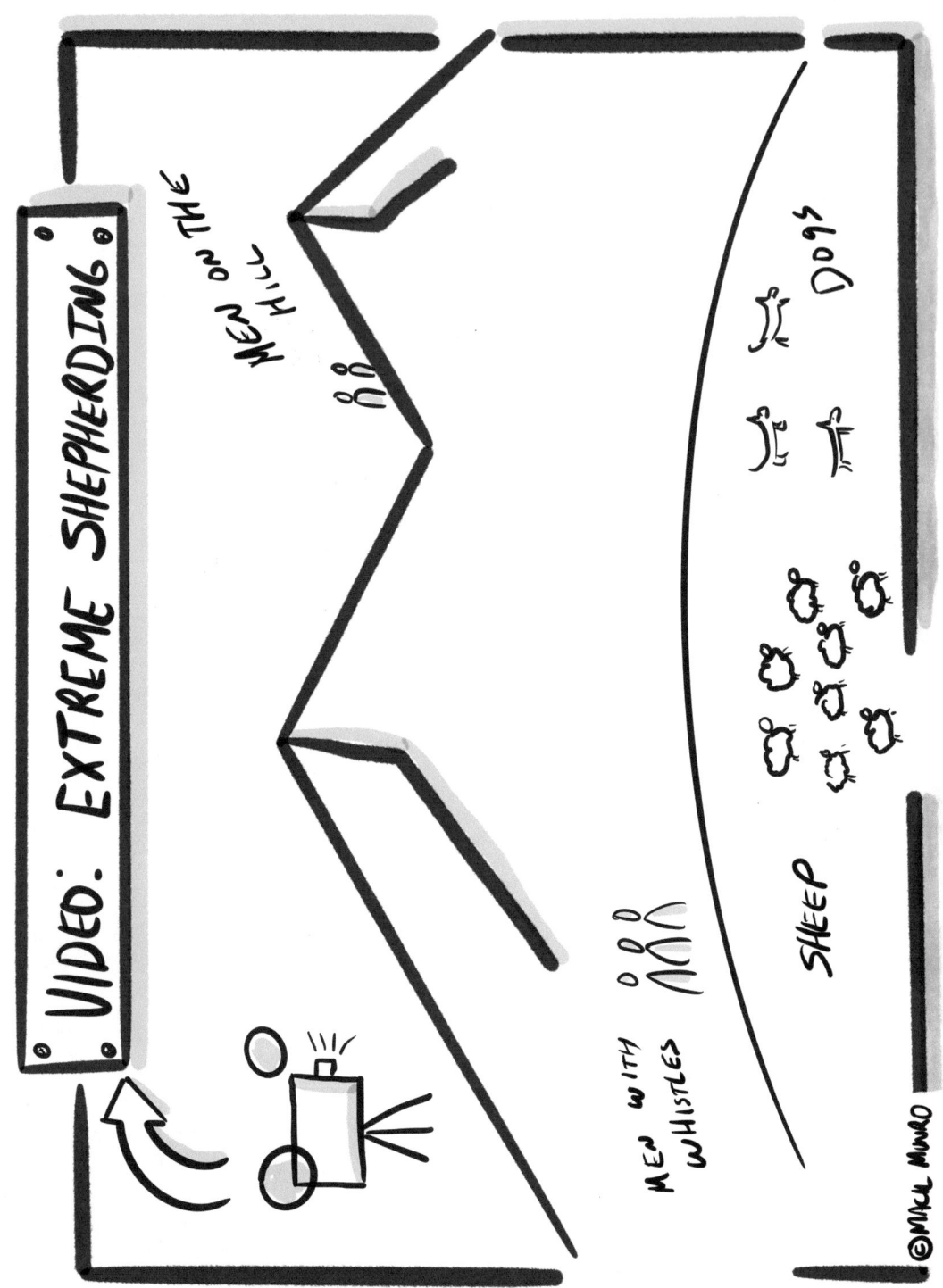

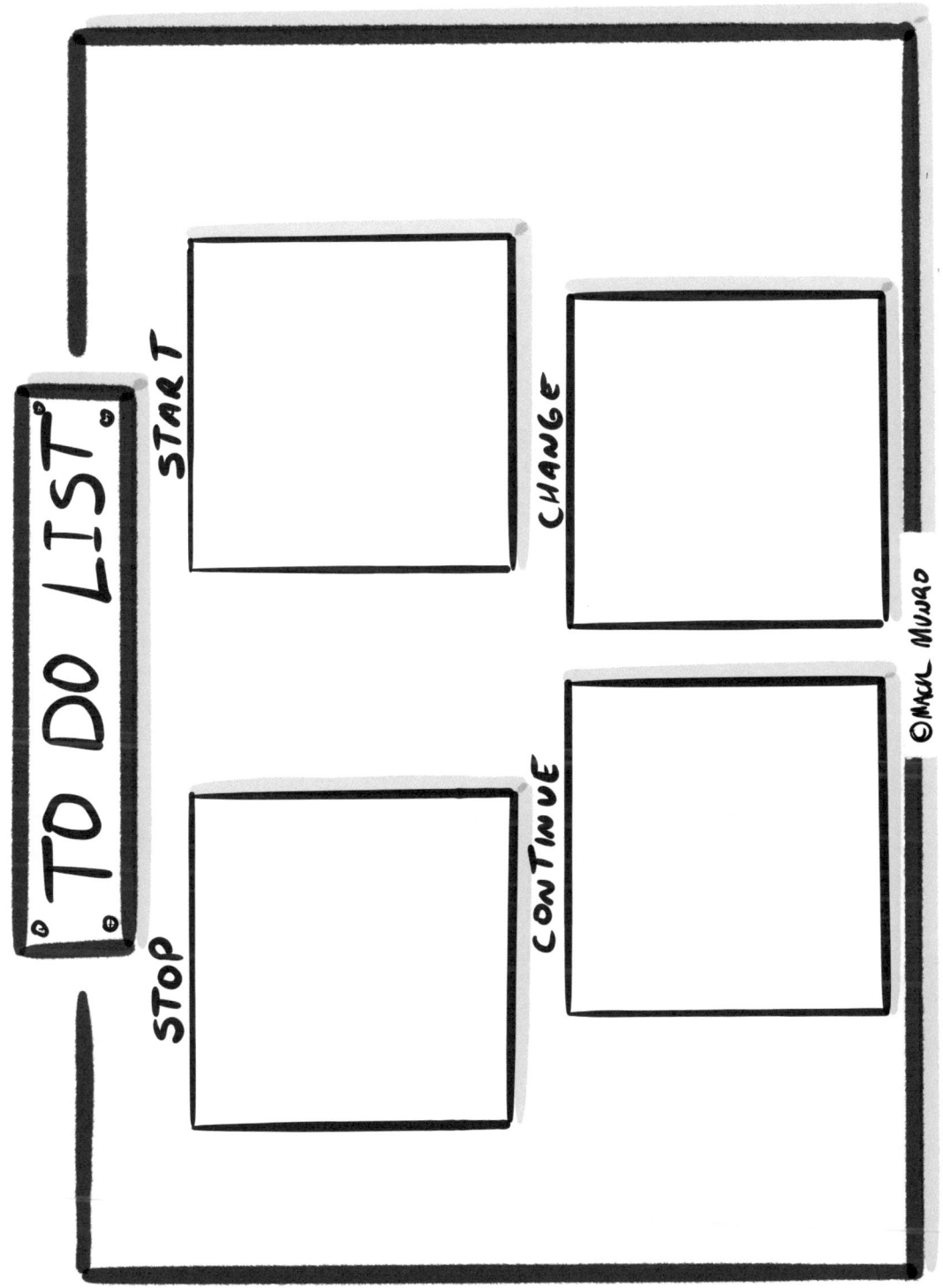

THE ART OF BEING A GREAT BOSS

Notes

Session 3

Building Relationships for Results – Part 1

Building Relationships for Results is designed to show you the importance of good communication, your default behavioral style, and how to build rapport with others.

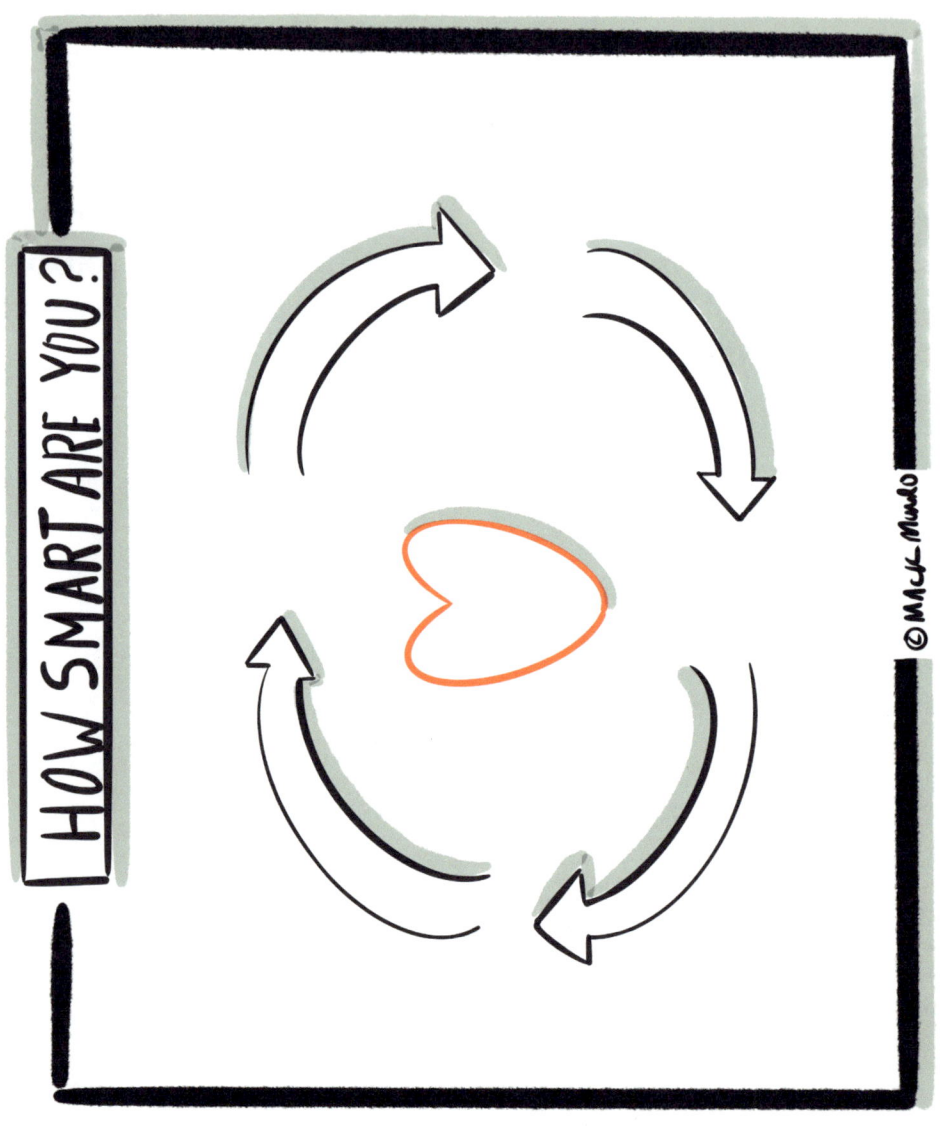

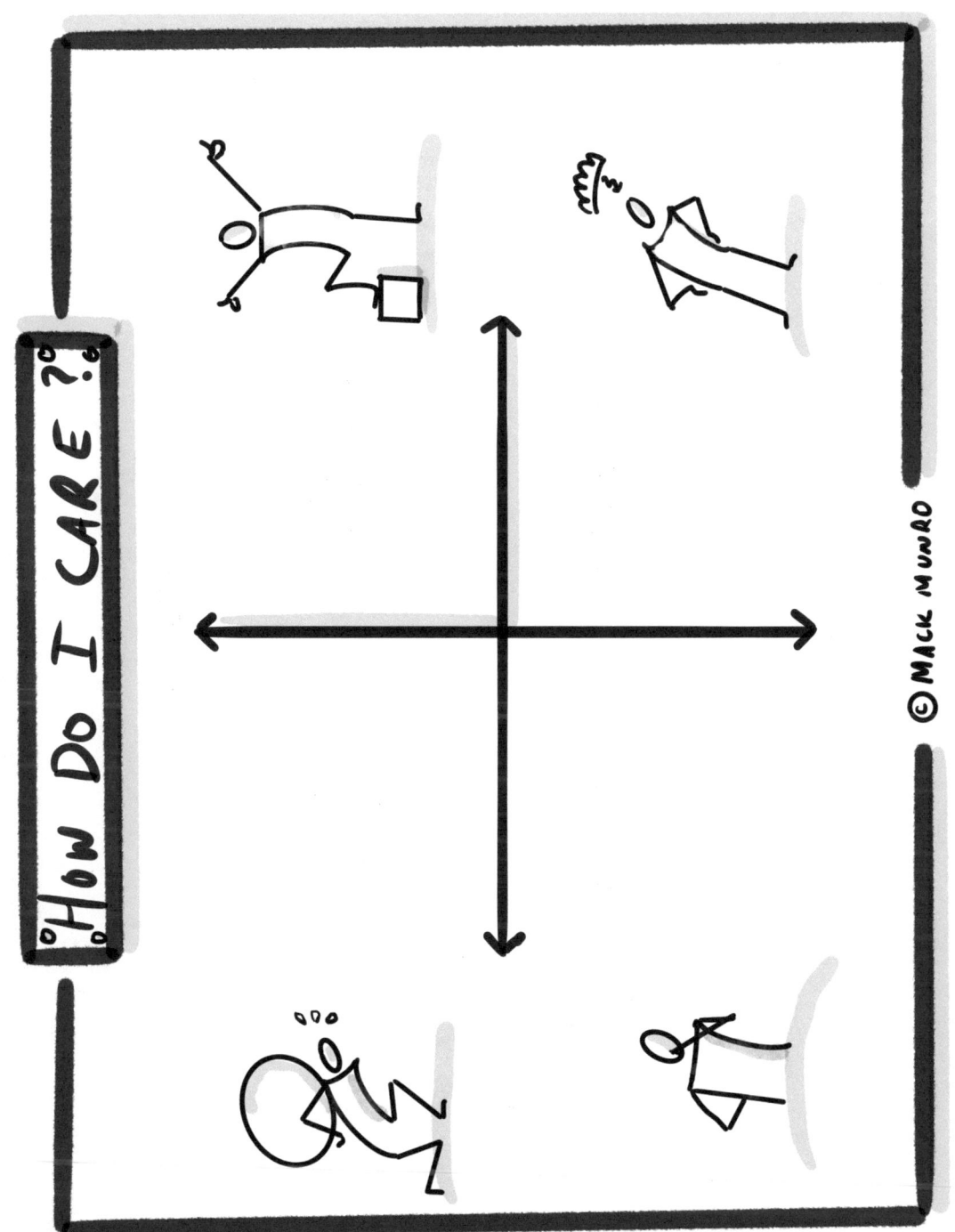

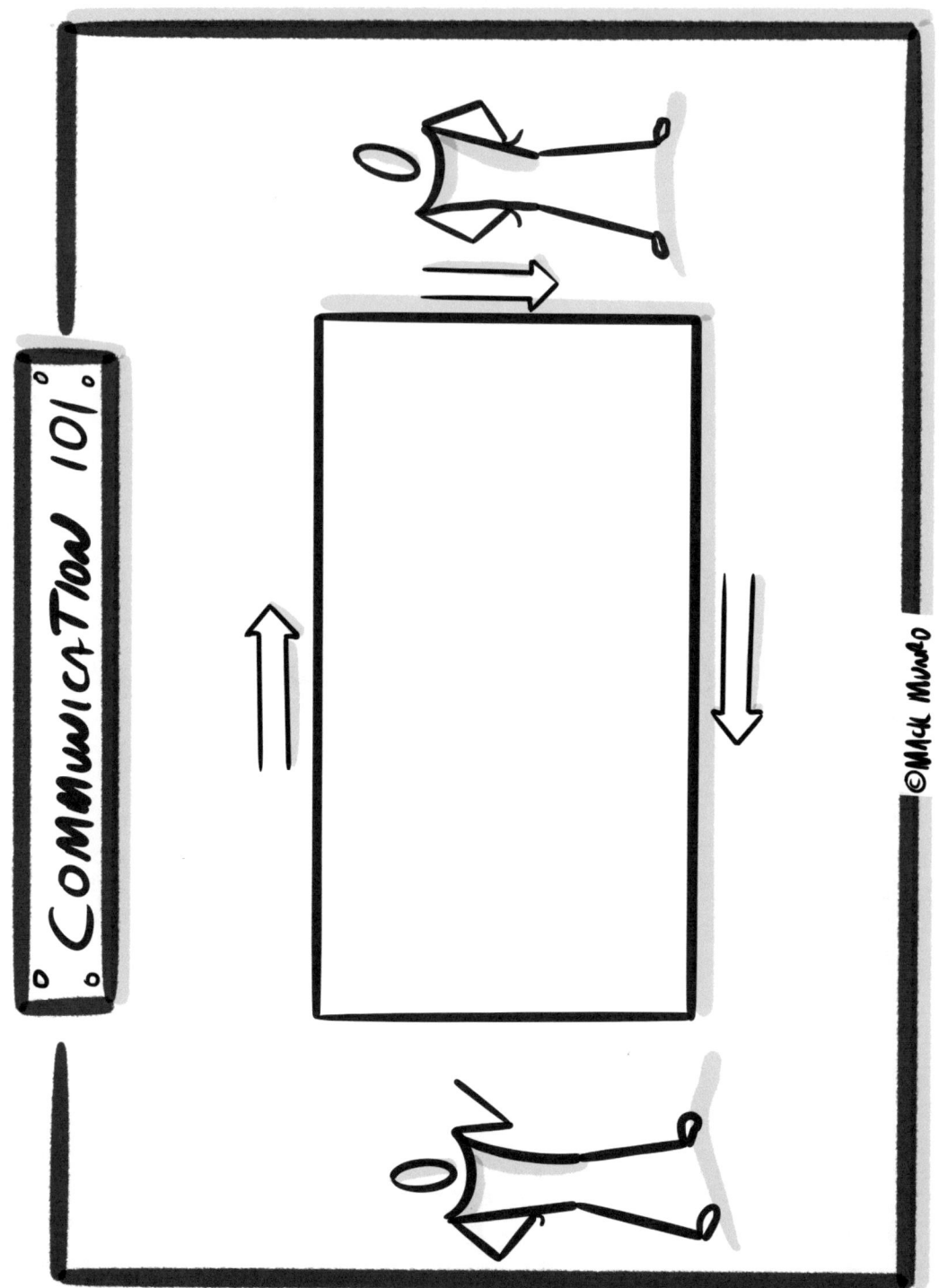

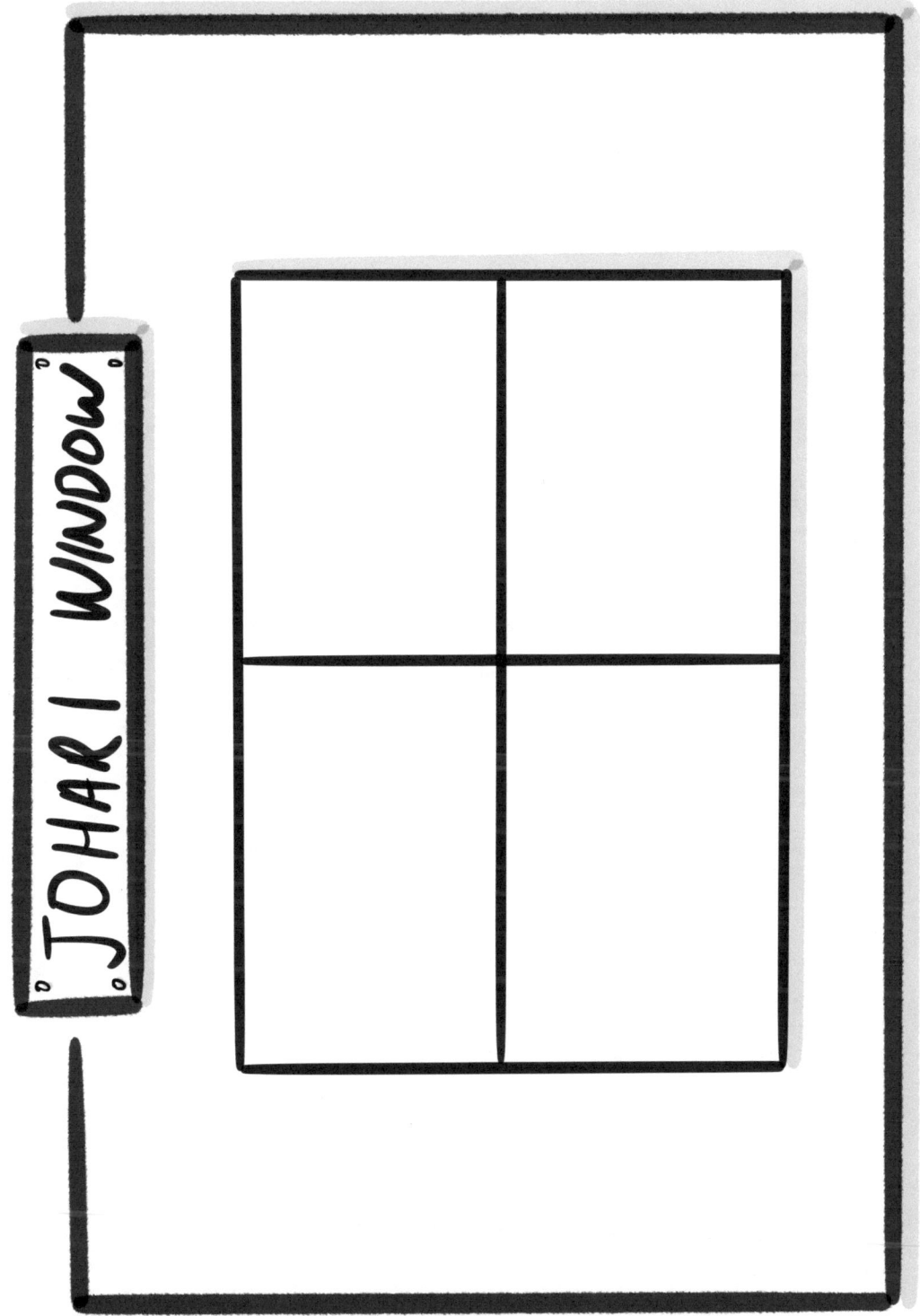

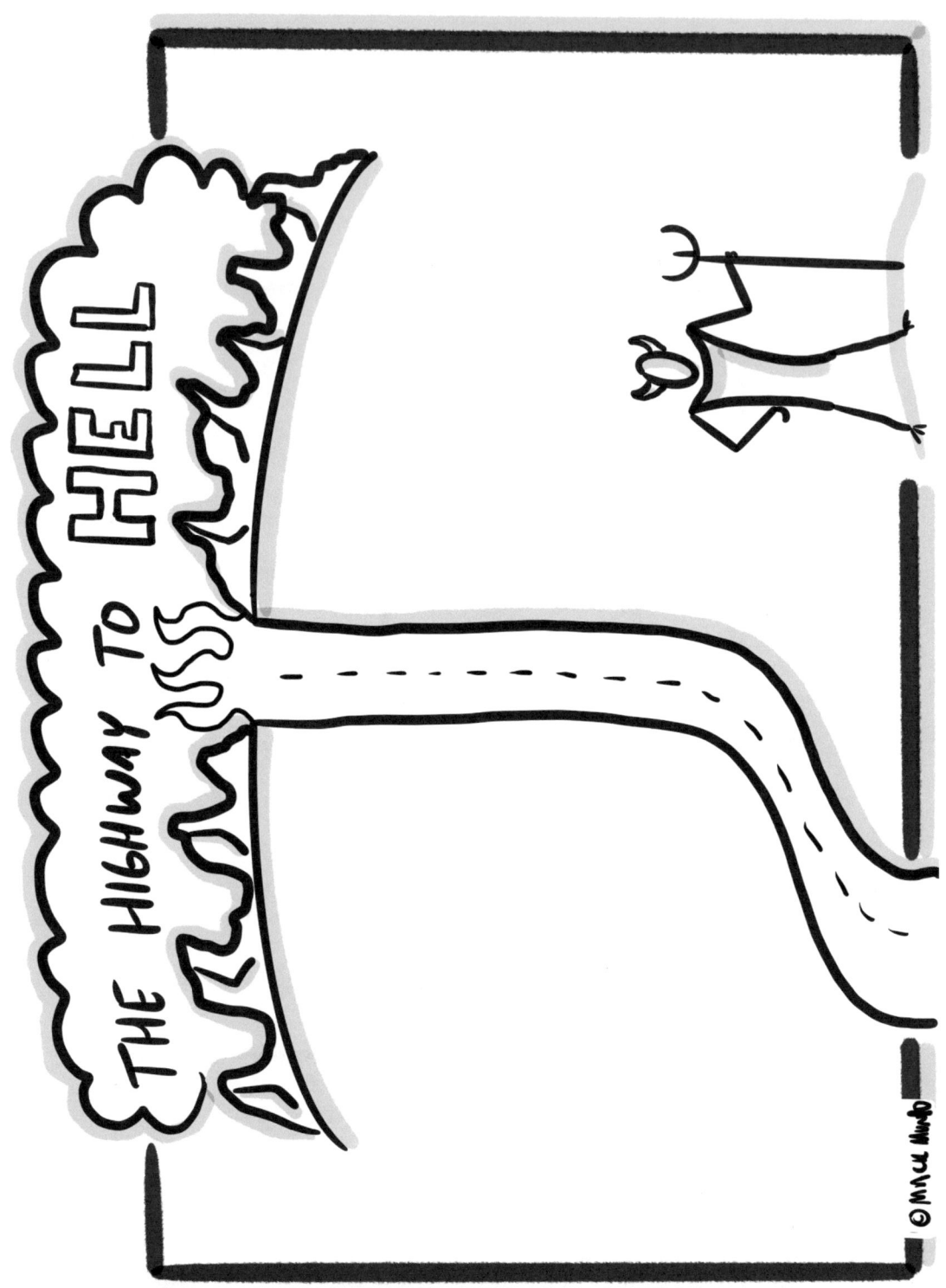

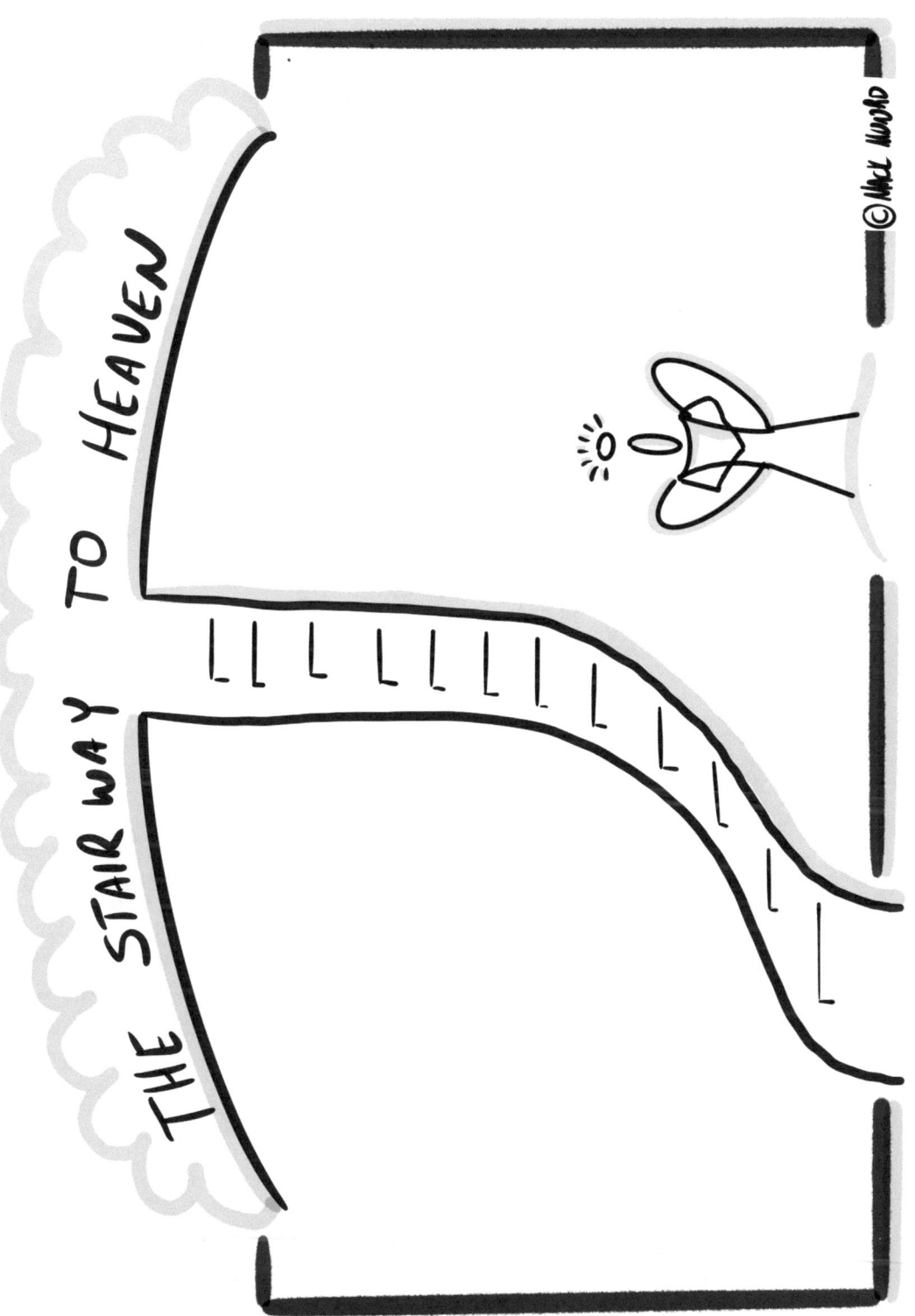

Communication Strategies

Active Listening
1. _____
2. _____
3. _____

Decoding

1. The Curse of _____
2. Know Your _____

Encoding

© Mack Munro

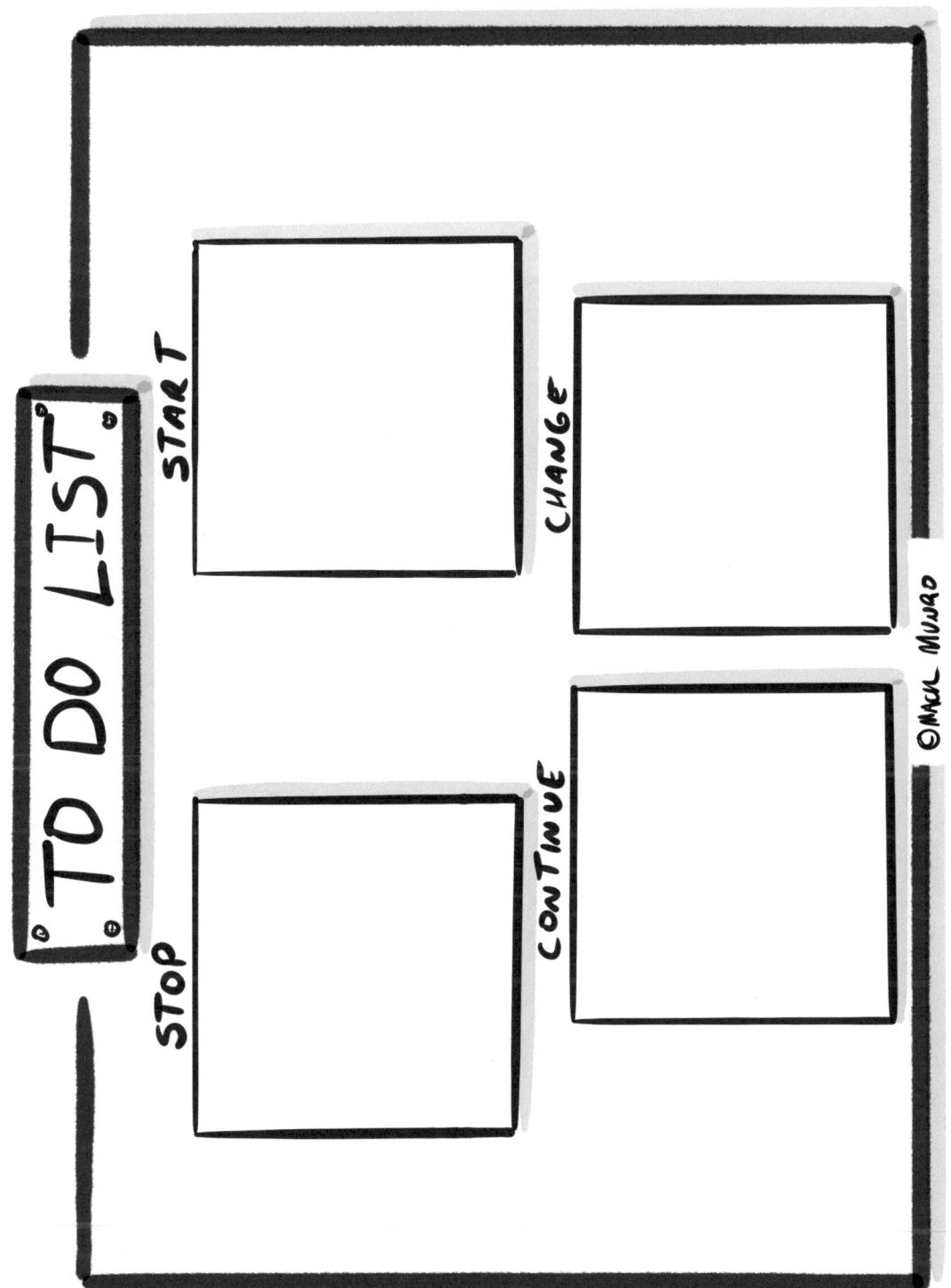

Notes

Session 4

Building Relationships for Results – Part 2

Building Relationships for Results is designed to show you the importance of good communication, your default behavioral style, and how to build rapport with others.

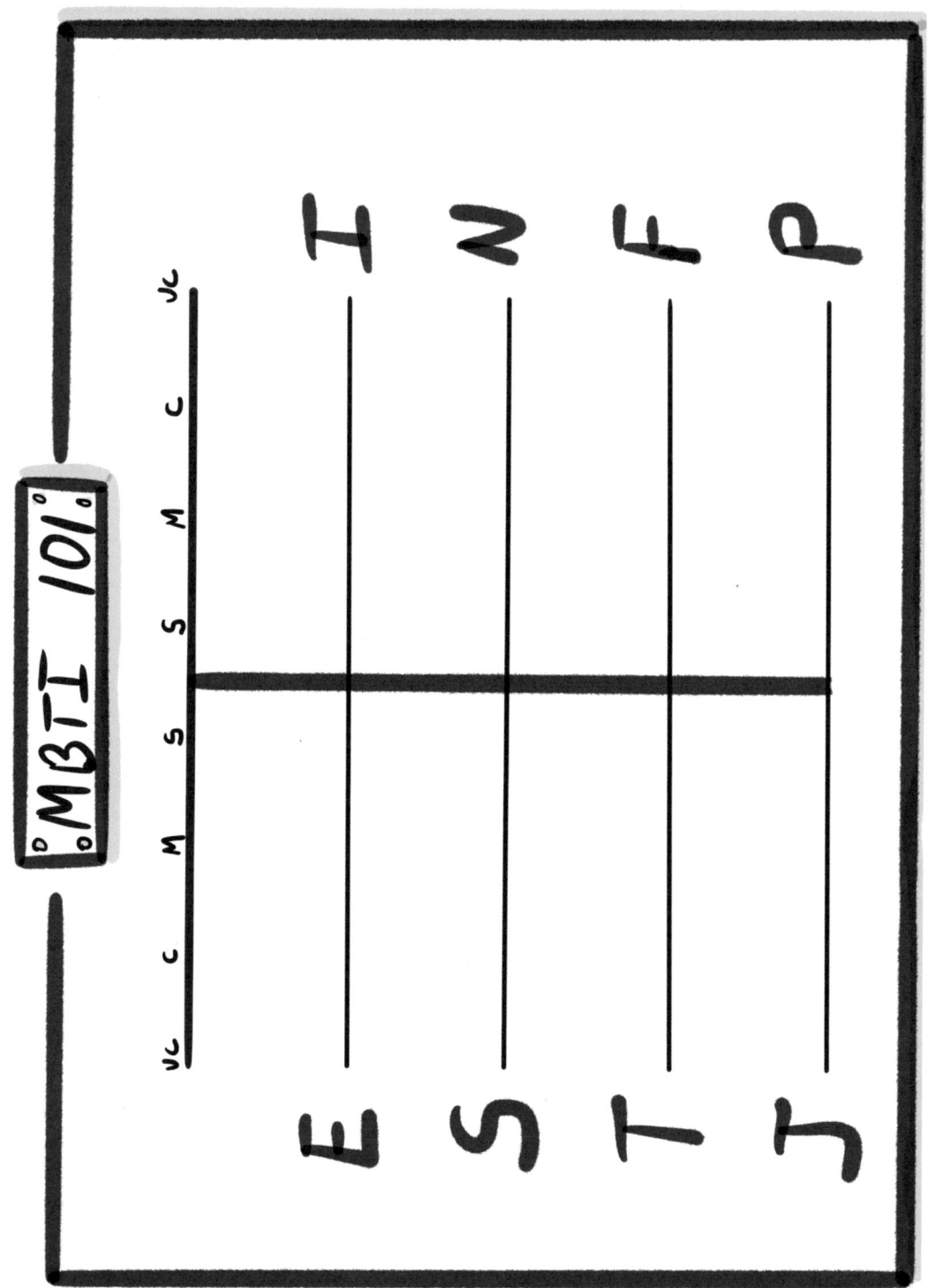

TYPE TO TEMPERAMENT

ENTJ
ENTP
INTJ
INTP

ESTP
ESFP
ISTP
ISFP

NF	NT
SJ	SP

ENFJ
ENFP
INFJ
INFP

ESTJ
ESFJ
ISTJ
ISFJ

© Mack Munro

THE ART OF BEING A GREAT BOSS | 29

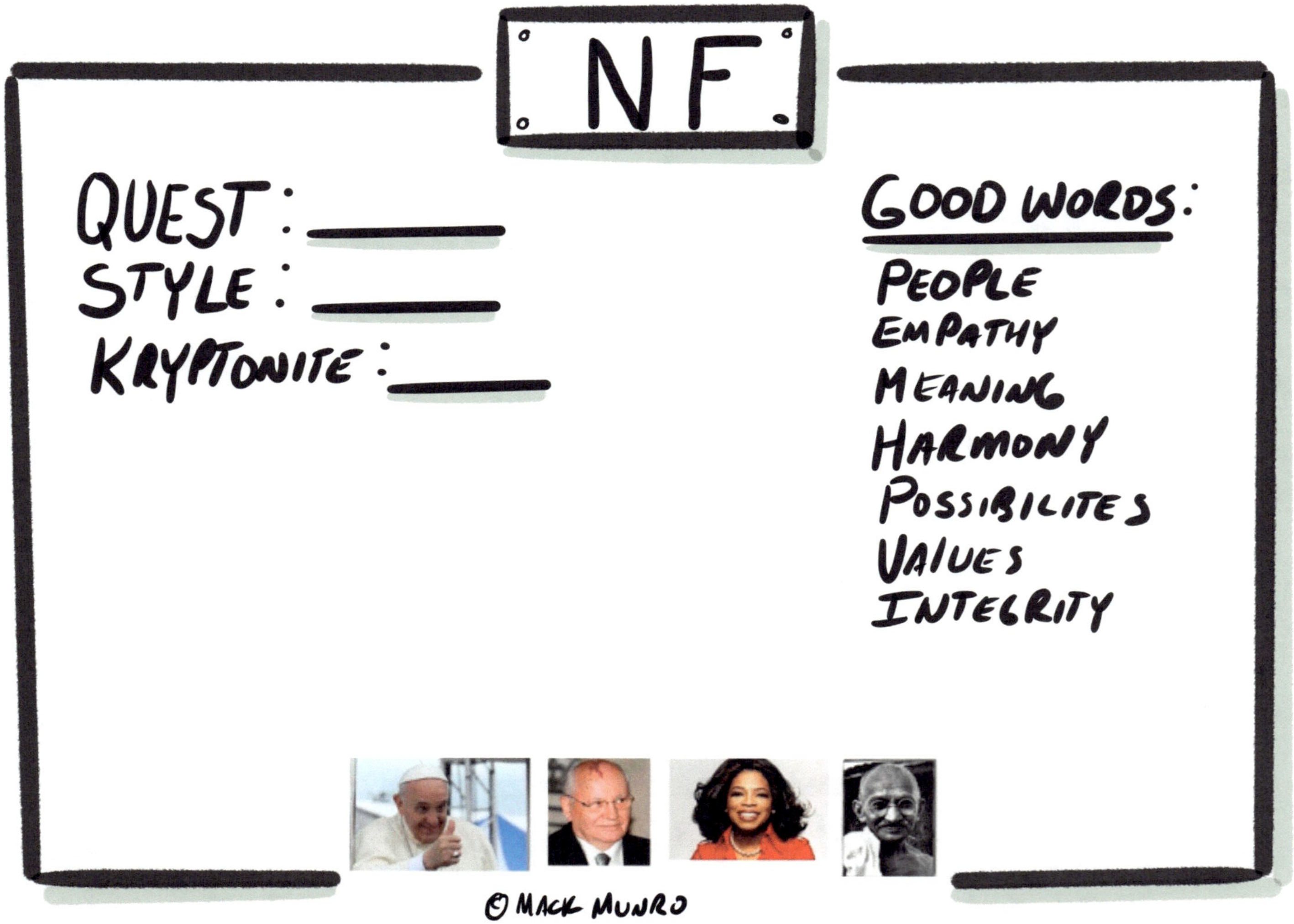

NF

GOOD WORDS:
- PEOPLE
- EMPATHY
- MEANING
- HARMONY
- POSSIBILITIES
- VALUES
- INTEGRITY

QUEST: _____
STYLE: _____
KRYPTONITE: _____

© MACK MUNRO

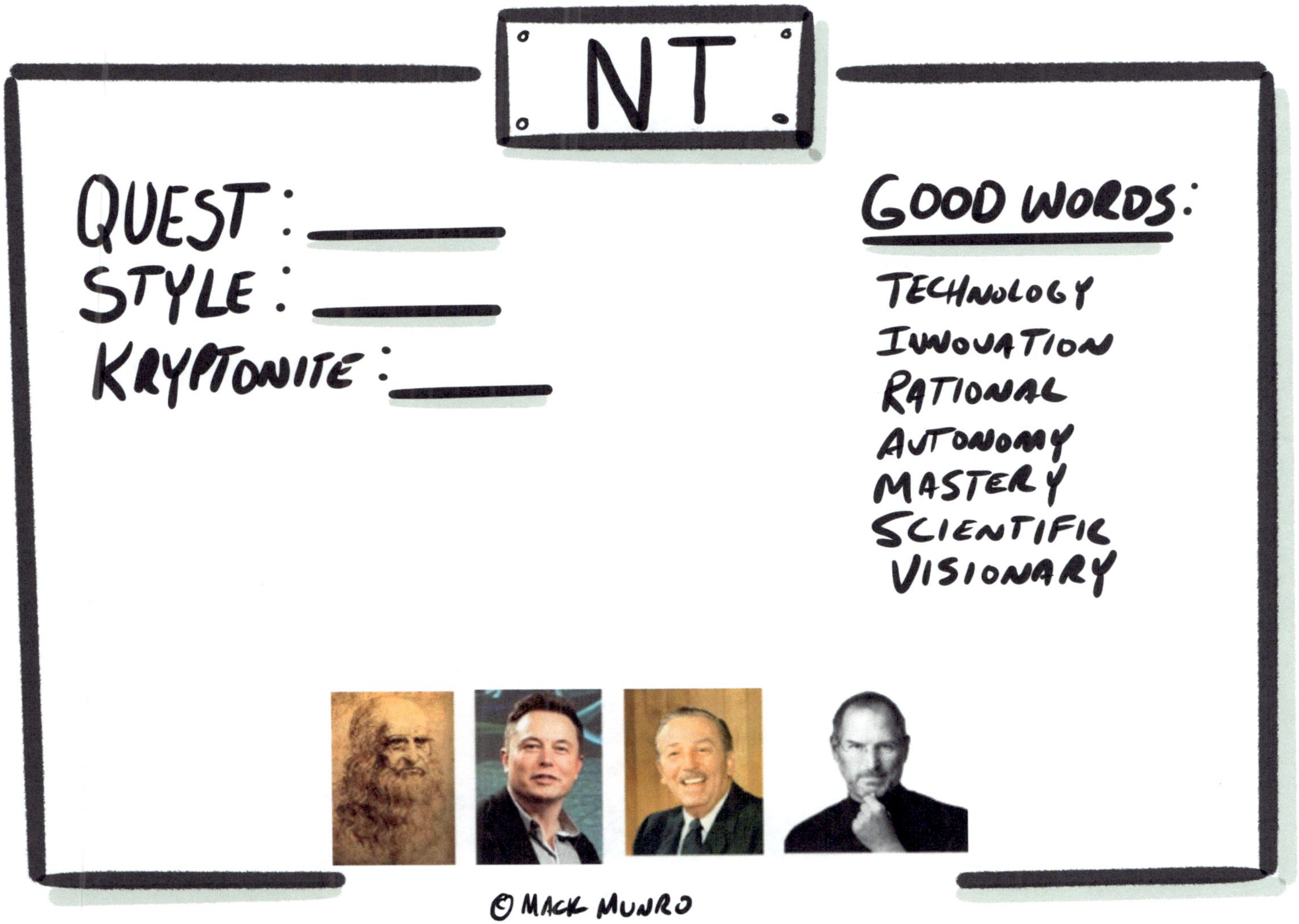

NT

GOOD WORDS:
- TECHNOLOGY
- INNOVATION
- RATIONAL
- AUTONOMY
- MASTERY
- SCIENTIFIC
- VISIONARY

QUEST: ___
STYLE: ___
KRYPTONITE: ___

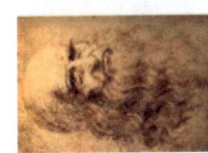

© MACK MUNRO

GOOD WORDS:
- RESPONSIBILITY
- SERVICE
- PROCEDURES
- LISTS
- SENSE OF BELONGING
- STANDARD WORK
- ACCOUNTABILITY

SJ

QUEST: _____
STYLE: _____
KRYPTONITE: _____

© MACK MUNRO

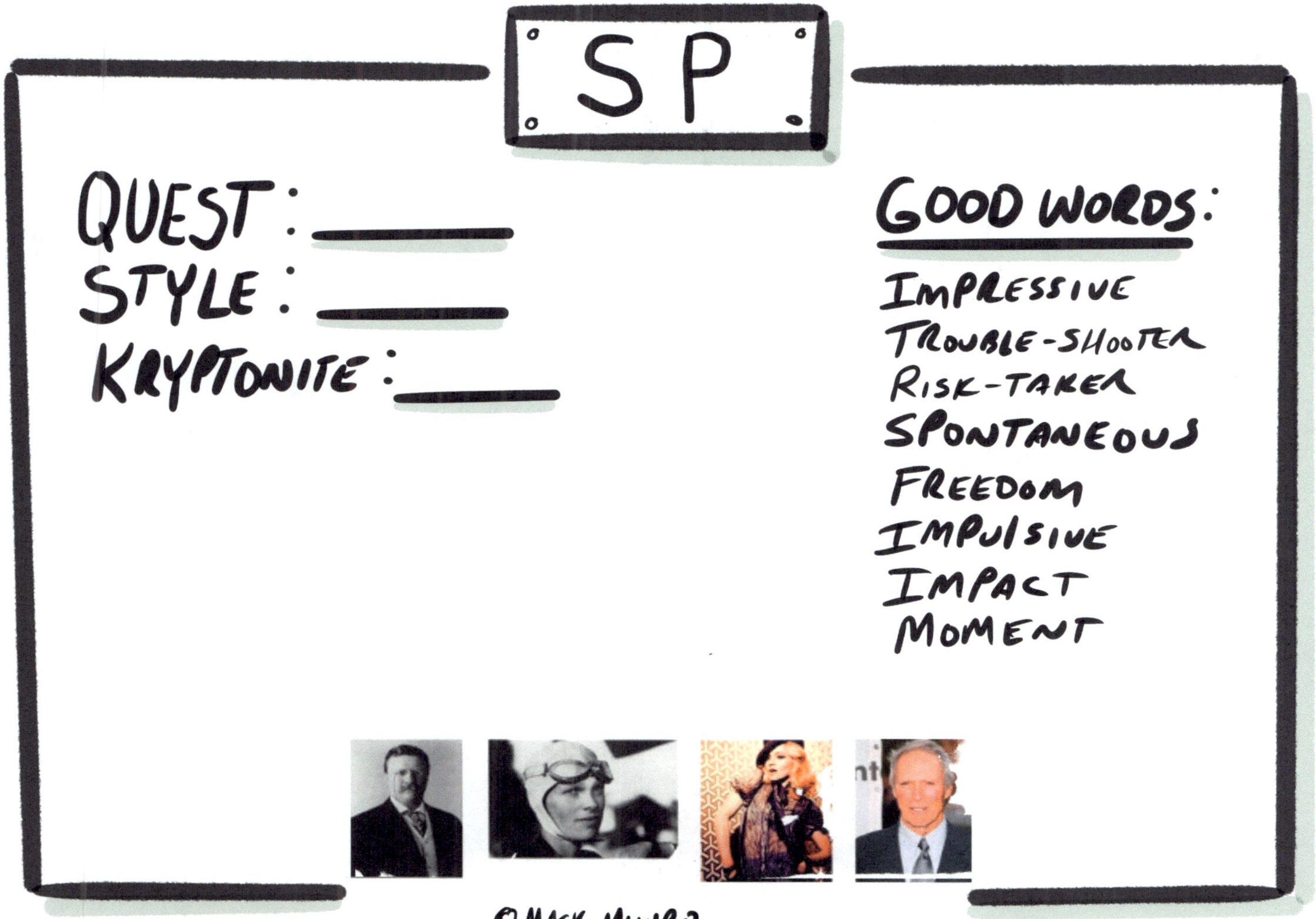

SP

GOOD WORDS:
- IMPRESSIVE
- TROUBLE-SHOOTER
- RISK-TAKER
- SPONTANEOUS
- FREEDOM
- IMPULSIVE
- IMPACT
- MOMENT

QUEST: ___
STYLE: ___
KRYPTONITE: ___

© MACK MUNRO

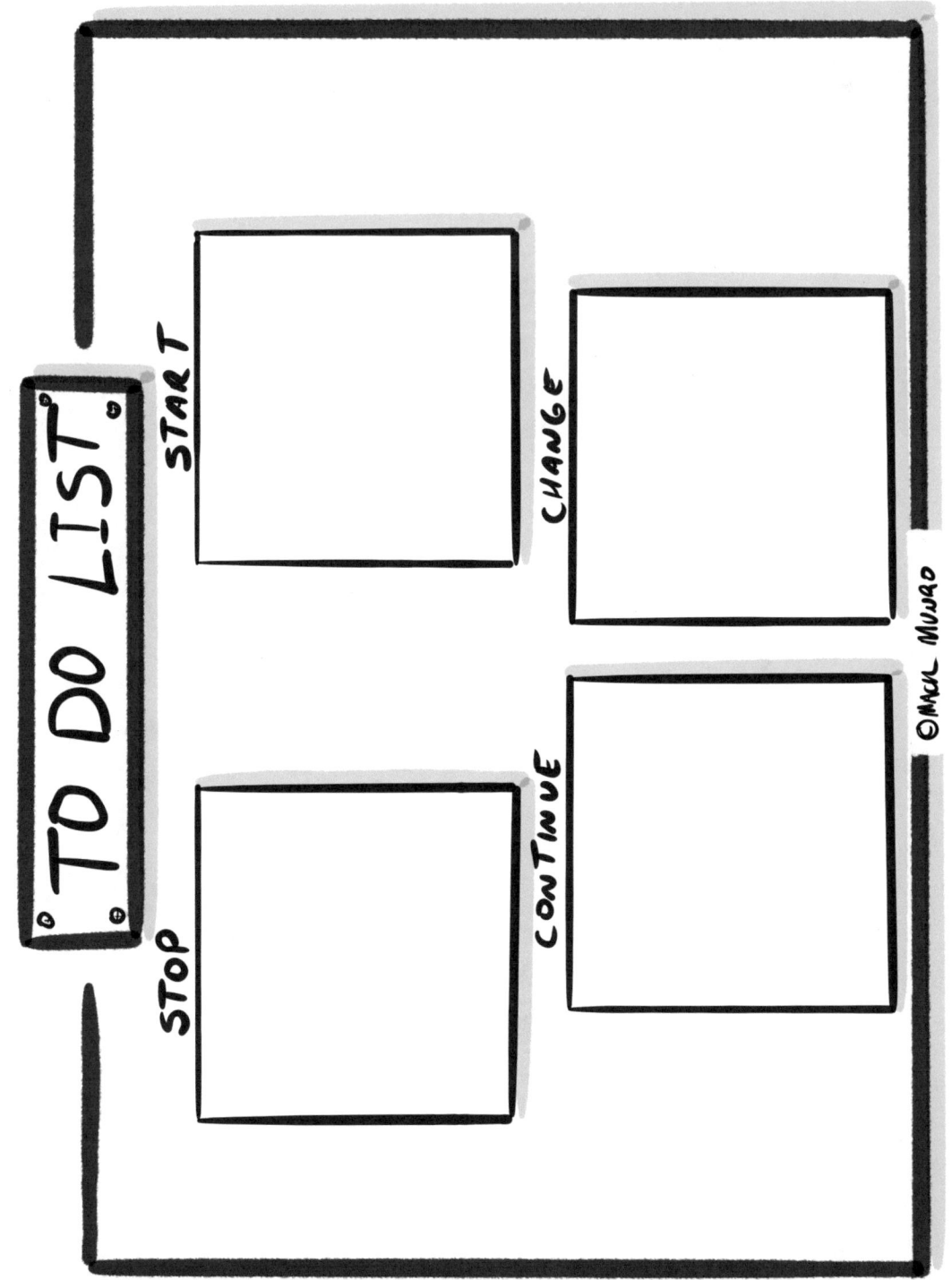

Session 5

Building Relationships for Results – Part 3

Building Relationships for Results is designed to show you the importance of good communication, your default behavioral style, and how to build rapport with others.

CONFLICT

Conflict: When what I ___ is not what I'm currently ___.

Respect: People are taking ___ me.

© Mack Munro

NF IN CONFLICT

IF THEY WANT: _____

YOU WILL SEE: _____

BUT INSTEAD GET: _____

WHICH YOU CAN FIX BY: _____

© Marc Muro

THE ART OF BEING A GREAT BOSS | 37

NT IN CONFLICT

IF THEY WANT: _____

YOU WILL SEE: _____

BUT INSTEAD GET: _____

WHICH YOU CAN FIX BY: _____

© Mack Munro

SJ IN CONFLICT

IF THEY WANT: ___

YOU WILL SEE: ___

BUT INSTEAD GET: ___

WHICH YOU CAN FIX BY: ___

© Mack Munro

SP IN CONFLICT

IF THEY WANT: _____

YOU WILL SEE: _____

BUT INSTEAD GET: _____

WHICH YOU CAN FIX BY: _____

© Mark Munro

THE ART OF BEING A GREAT BOSS

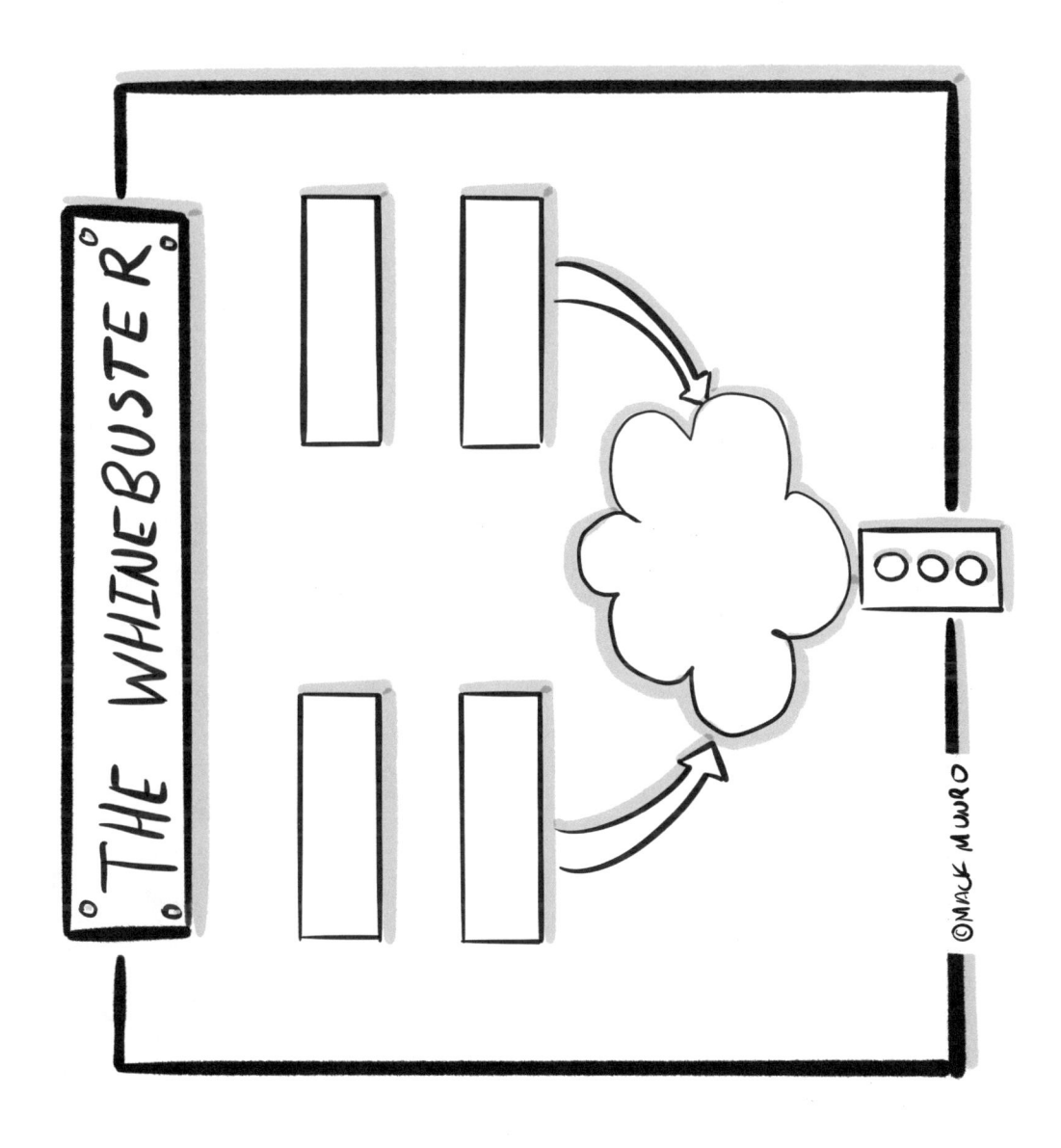

42 THE ART OF BEING A GREAT BOSS

Rules of Temperament

THE ART OF BEING A GREAT BOSS | 43

TO DO LIST

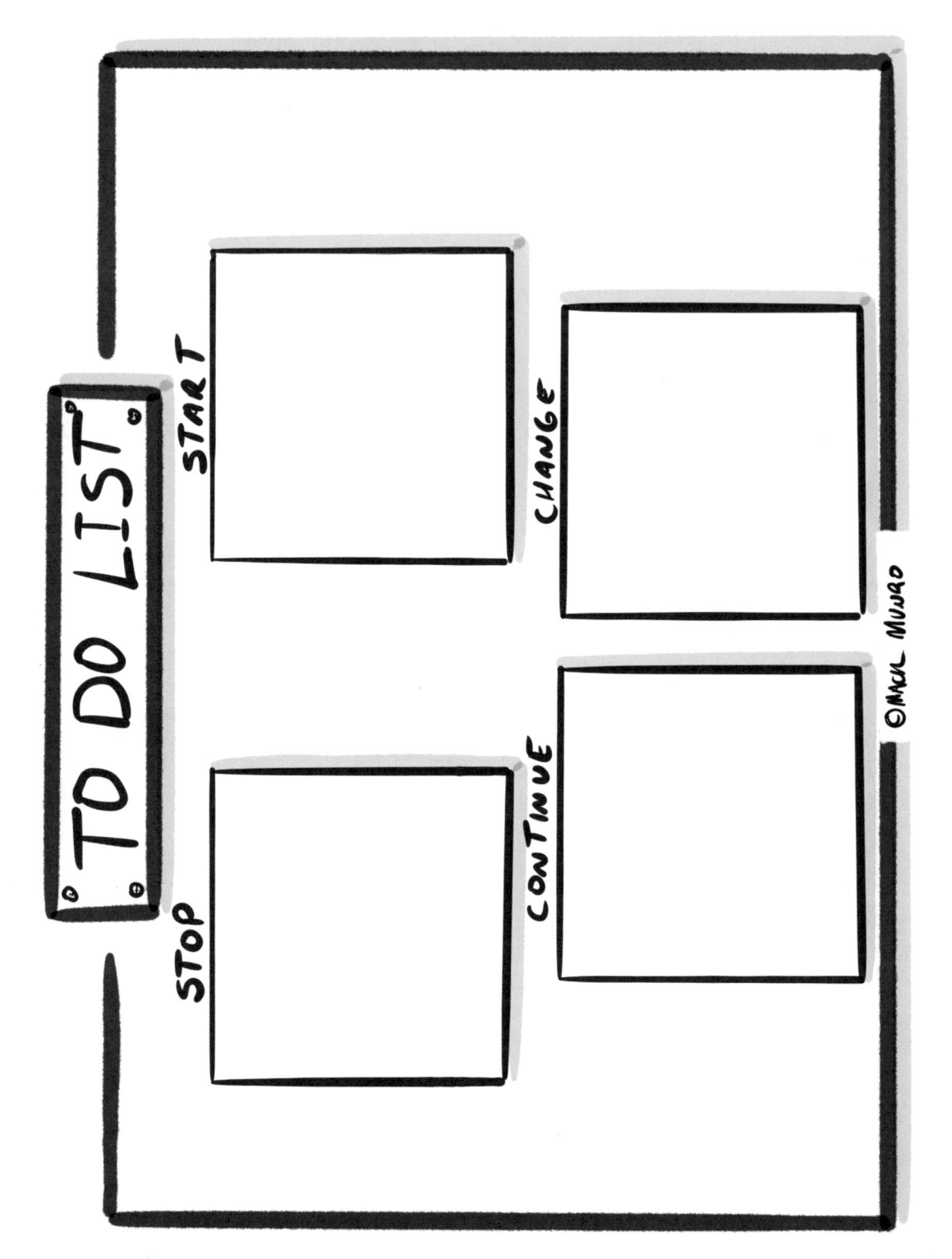

START	CHANGE
STOP	CONTINUE

© Neil Munro

Session 6

Driving Results – Part 1

Driving Results is designed to give you tools, and techniques to becoming an effective manager of performance.

46 | THE ART OF BEING A GREAT BOSS

FOCUS

	Very Clear	Clear	Moderate	Slight		Slight	Moderate	Clear	Very Clear	
Optimist	30	25	20	15	10	5	*Mindset / Focus*	5	10	15	20	25	30	Pessimist
Teamwork	30	25	20	15	10	5	*Work Style / Focus*	5	10	15	20	25	30	Individual
Emotional	30	25	20	15	10	5	*Relationship / Focus*	5	10	15	20	25	30	Rational
Visionary	30	25	20	15	10	5	*Perspective / Focus*	5	10	15	20	25	30	Realistic
Multi-Task	30	25	20	15	10	5	*Self-Structure / Focus*	5	10	15	20	25	30	Single-Task
Assertive	30	25	20	15	10	5	*Communication / Focus*	5	10	15	20	25	30	Reflective
	Very Clear	Clear	Moderate	Slight		Slight	Moderate	Clear	Very Clear	

© MICK MUNRO

THE ART OF BEING A GREAT BOSS | 47

Development Journey

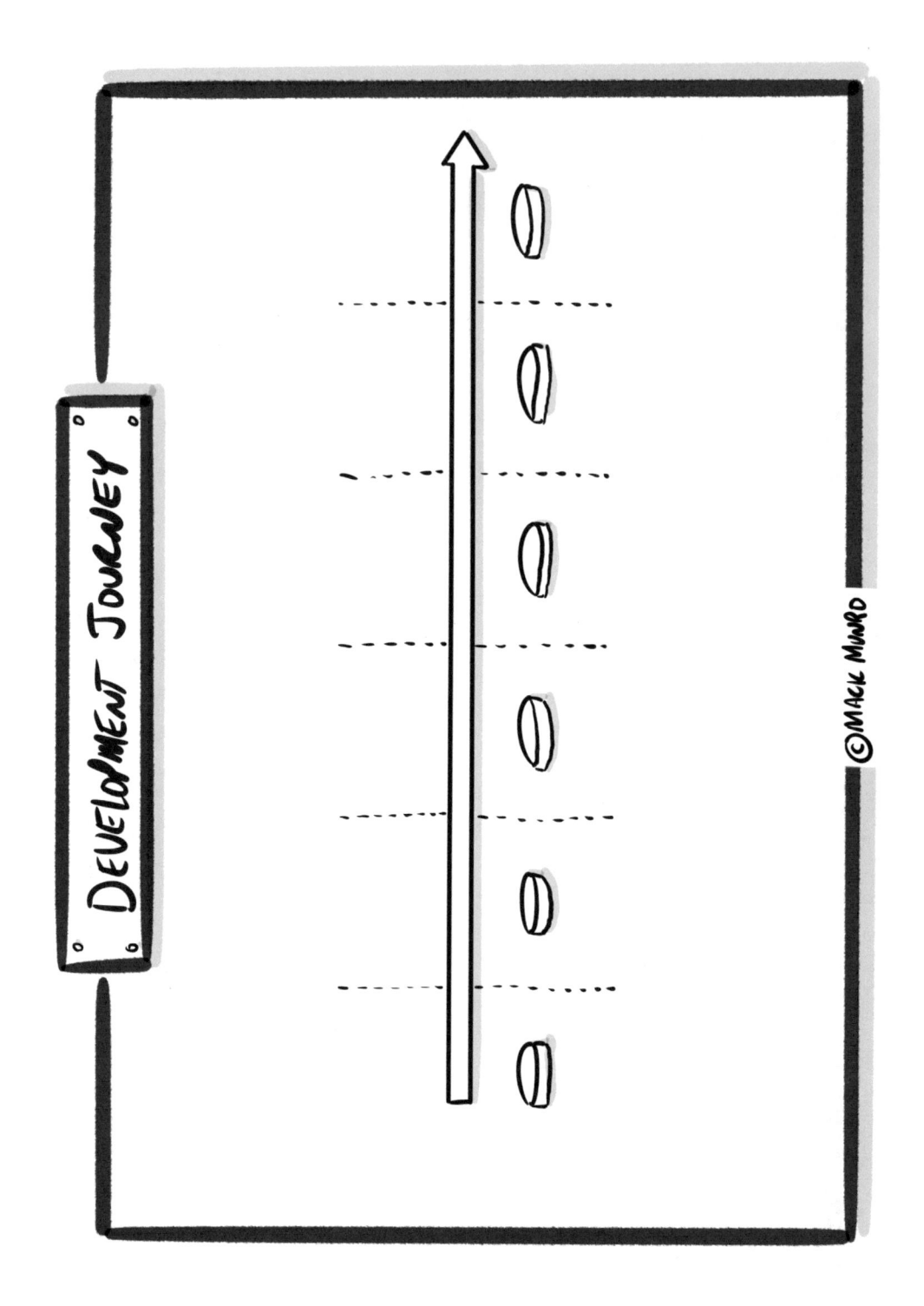

© Mack Munro

TO DO LIST

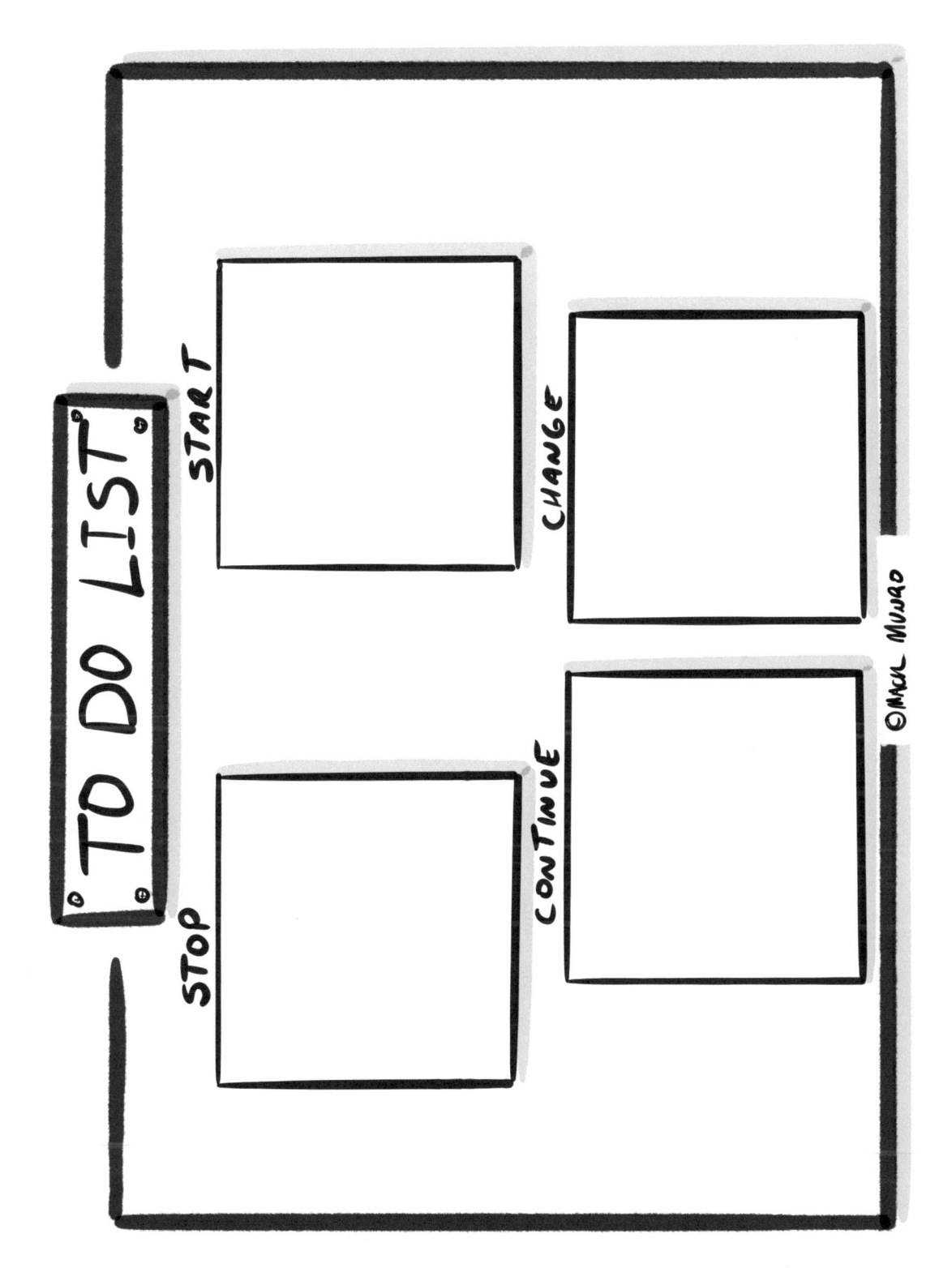

START

CHANGE

STOP

CONTINUE

THE ART OF BEING A GREAT BOSS

Notes

Session 7

Driving Results – Part 2

Driving Results is designed to give you tools, and techniques to becoming an effective manager of performance.

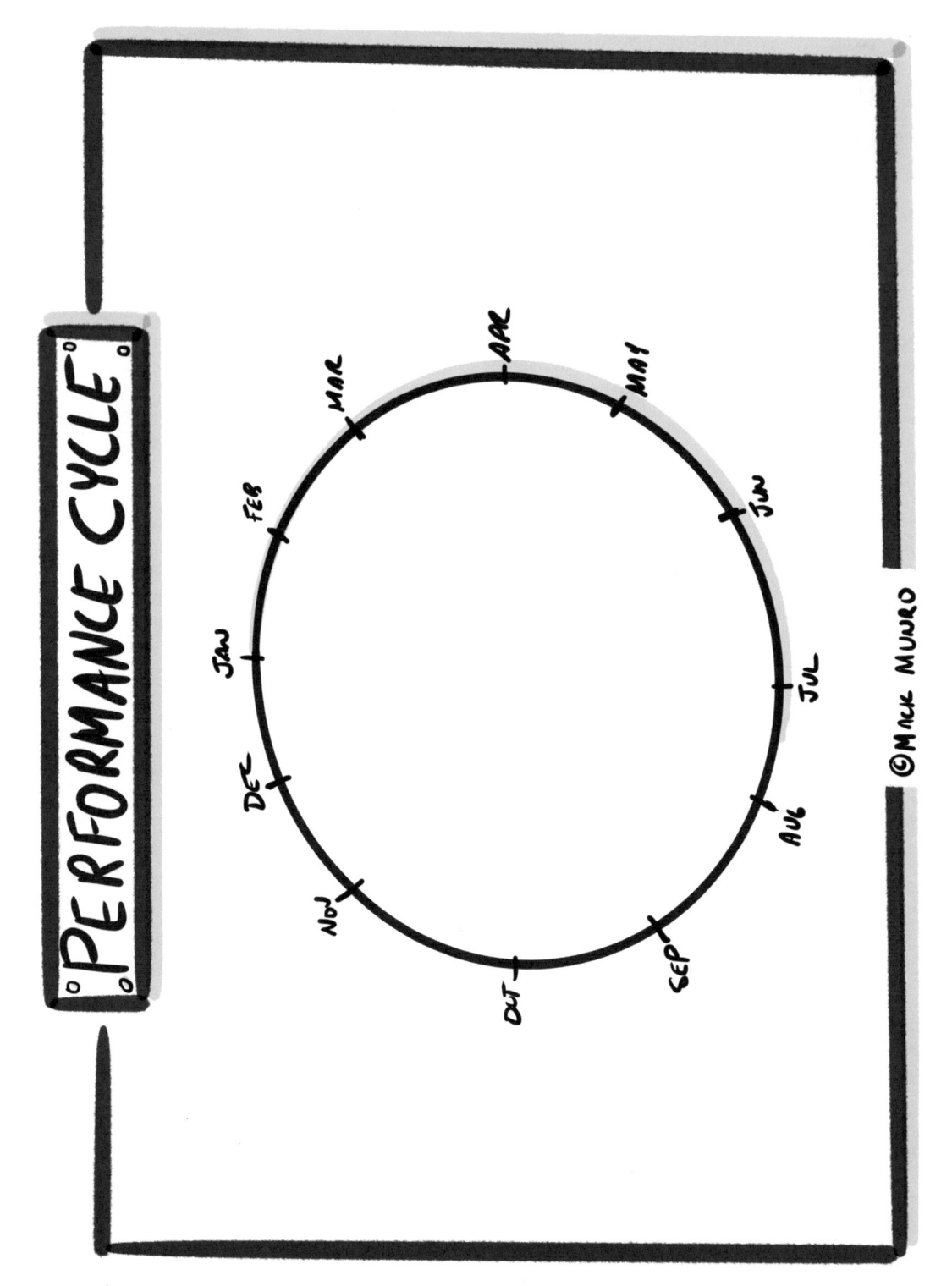

Performance Cycle

JAN • FEB • MAR • APR • MAY • JUN • JUL • AUG • SEP • OCT • NOV • DEC

© Mark Munro

THE ART OF BEING A GREAT BOSS

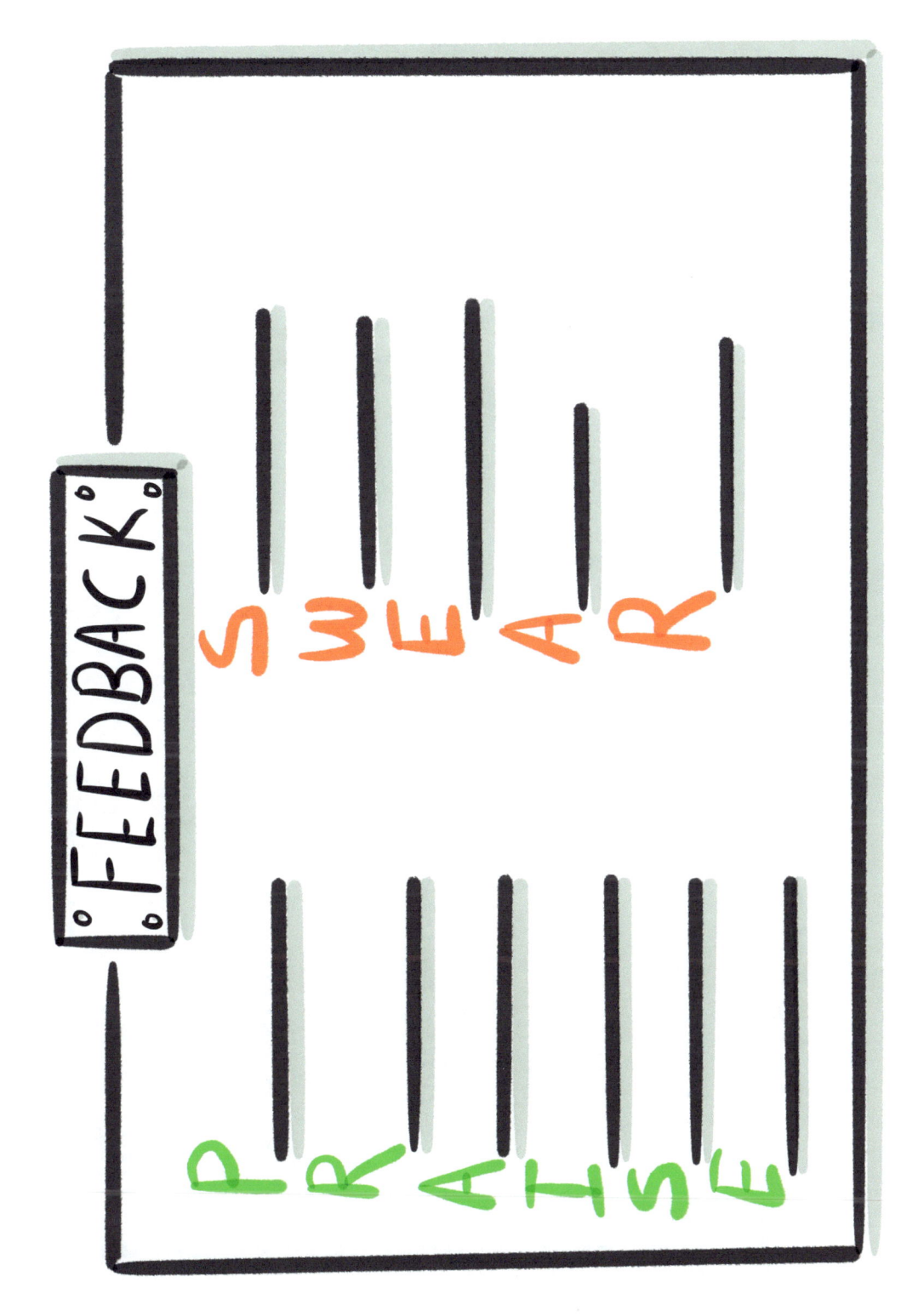

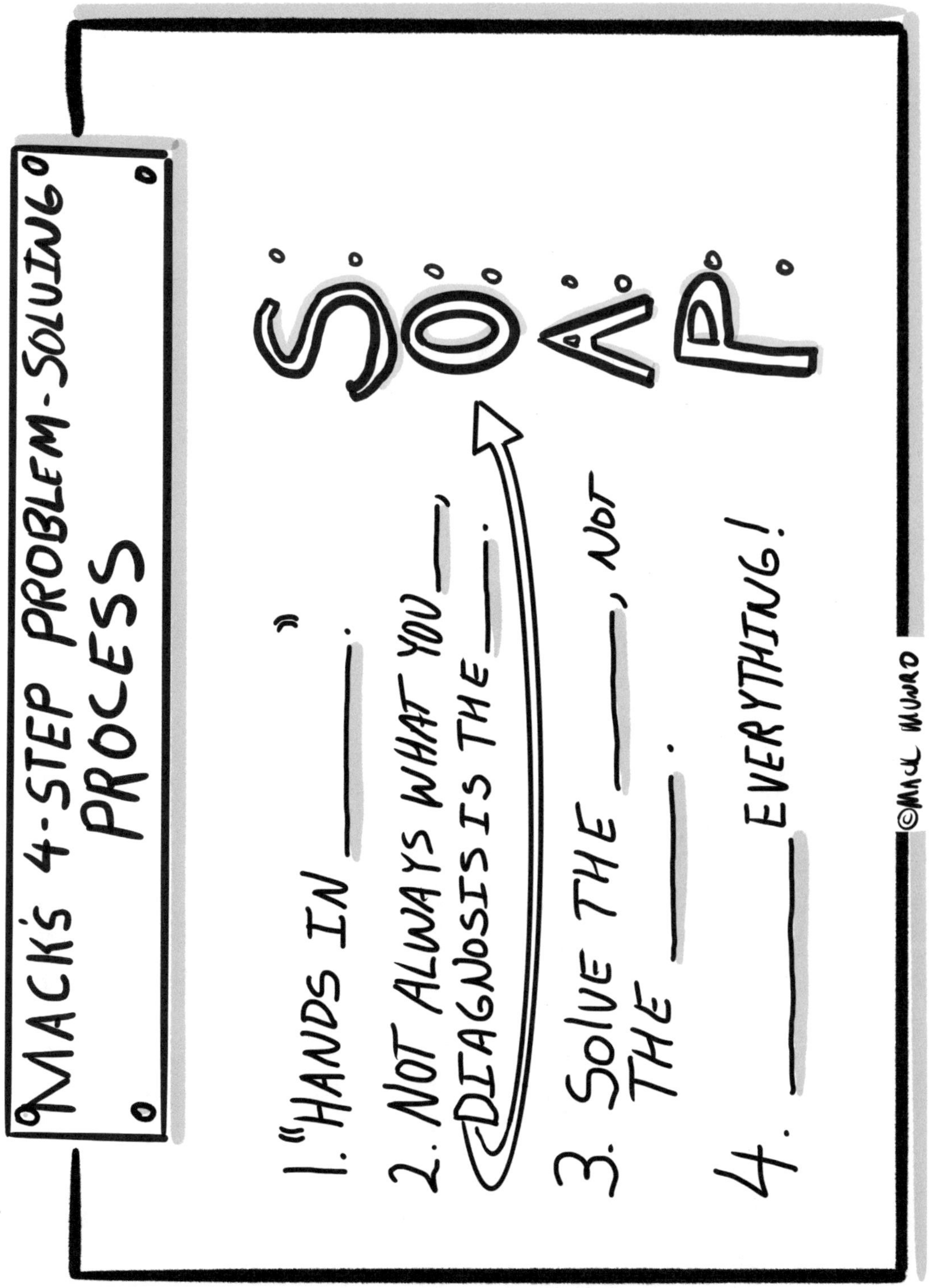

MACK'S 4-STEP PROBLEM-SOLVING PROCESS

S.O.A.P.

1. "HANDS IN ____"

2. NOT ALWAYS WHAT YOU ____, DIAGNOSIS IS THE ____

3. SOLVE THE ____, NOT THE ____.

4. ____ EVERYTHING!

©MACK MUNRO

Ted Has an "Attitude Problem"

1. Late 3x in last 2 weeks.
2. Overheard badmouthing you.
3. Told a customer to "F*** off" on the phone. (3 credible witnesses)
4. Seems apathetic and lethargic.

I don't have an attitude!

© Mark Munro

THE ART OF BEING A GREAT BOSS | 55

EVALUATION ERRORS

THE ART OF BEING A GREAT BOSS

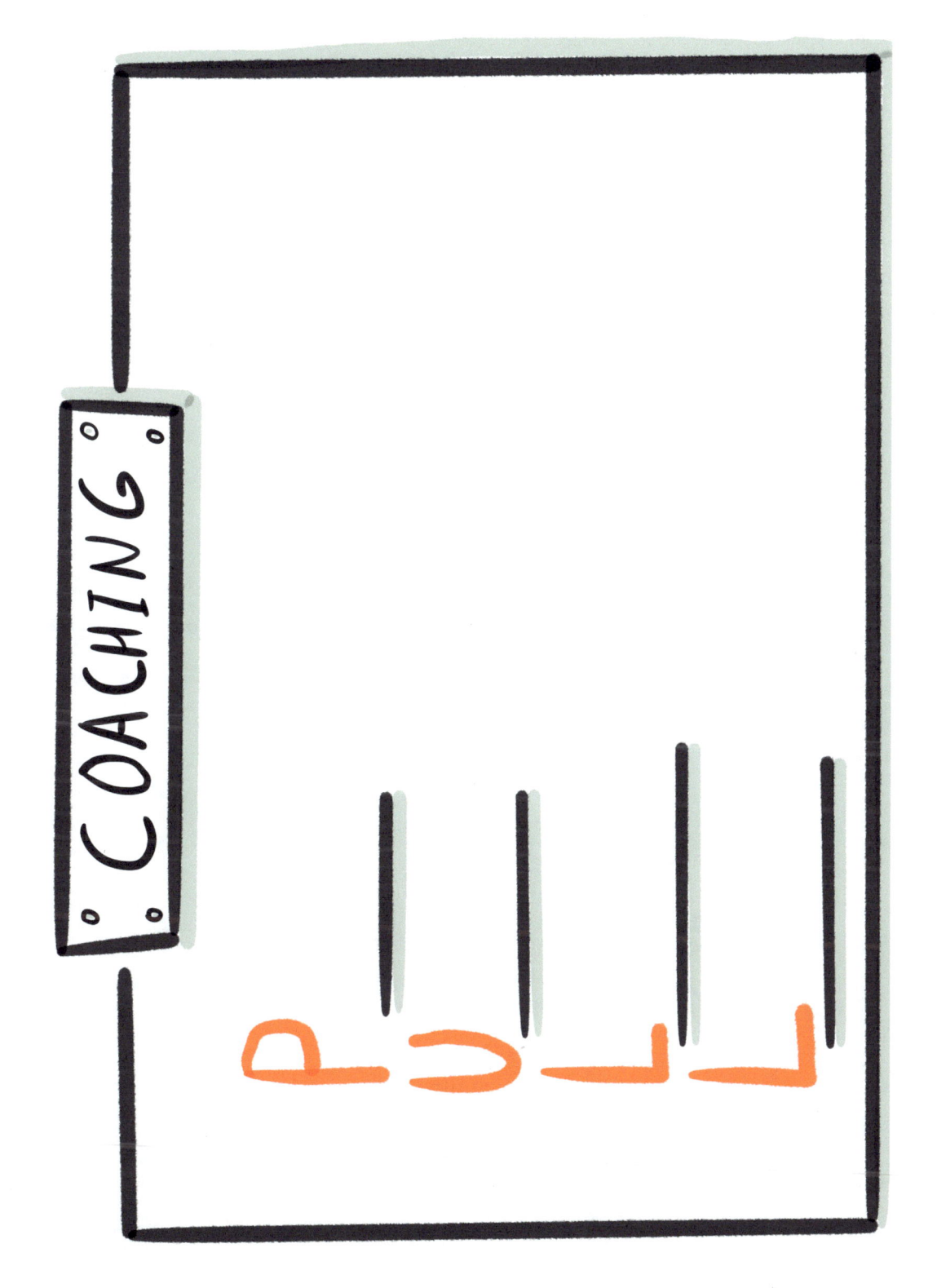

TO DO LIST

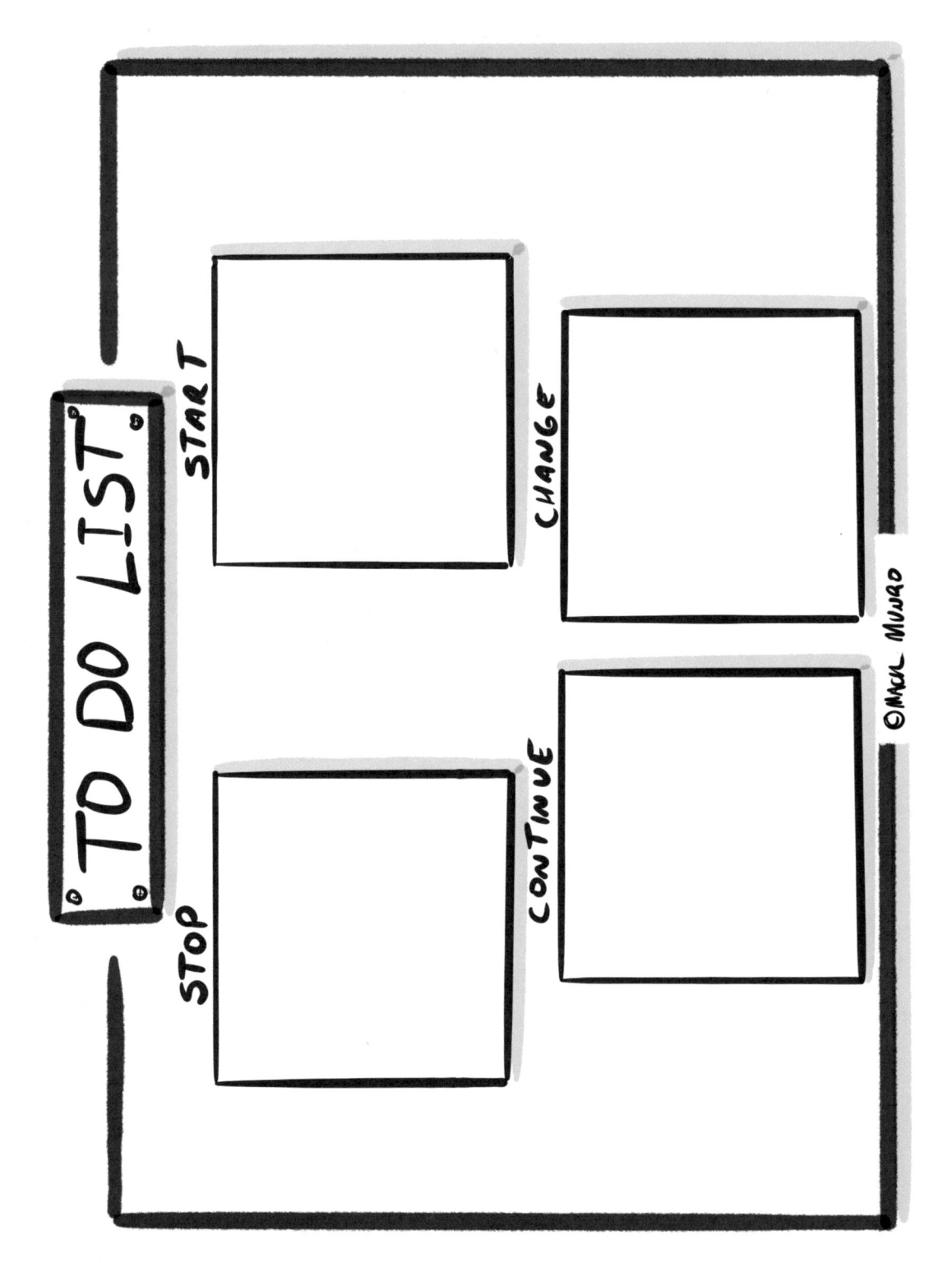

	START	CHANGE
	STOP	CONTINUE

©Mack Munro

Session 8

Driving Results – Part 3

Driving Results is designed to give you tools, and techniques to becoming an effective manager of performance.

60 | THE ART OF BEING A GREAT BOSS

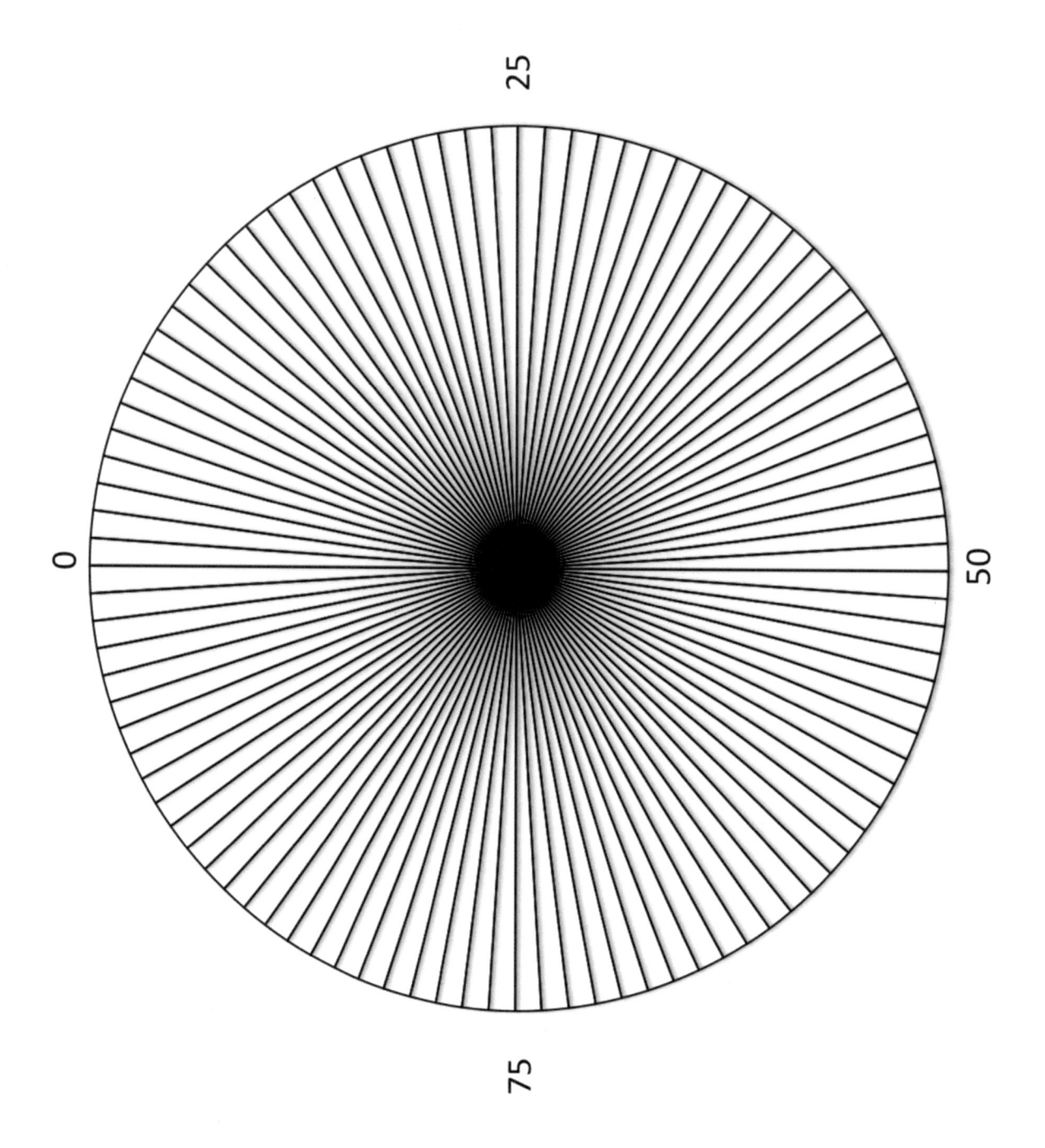

EMPLOYEE RESPONSES

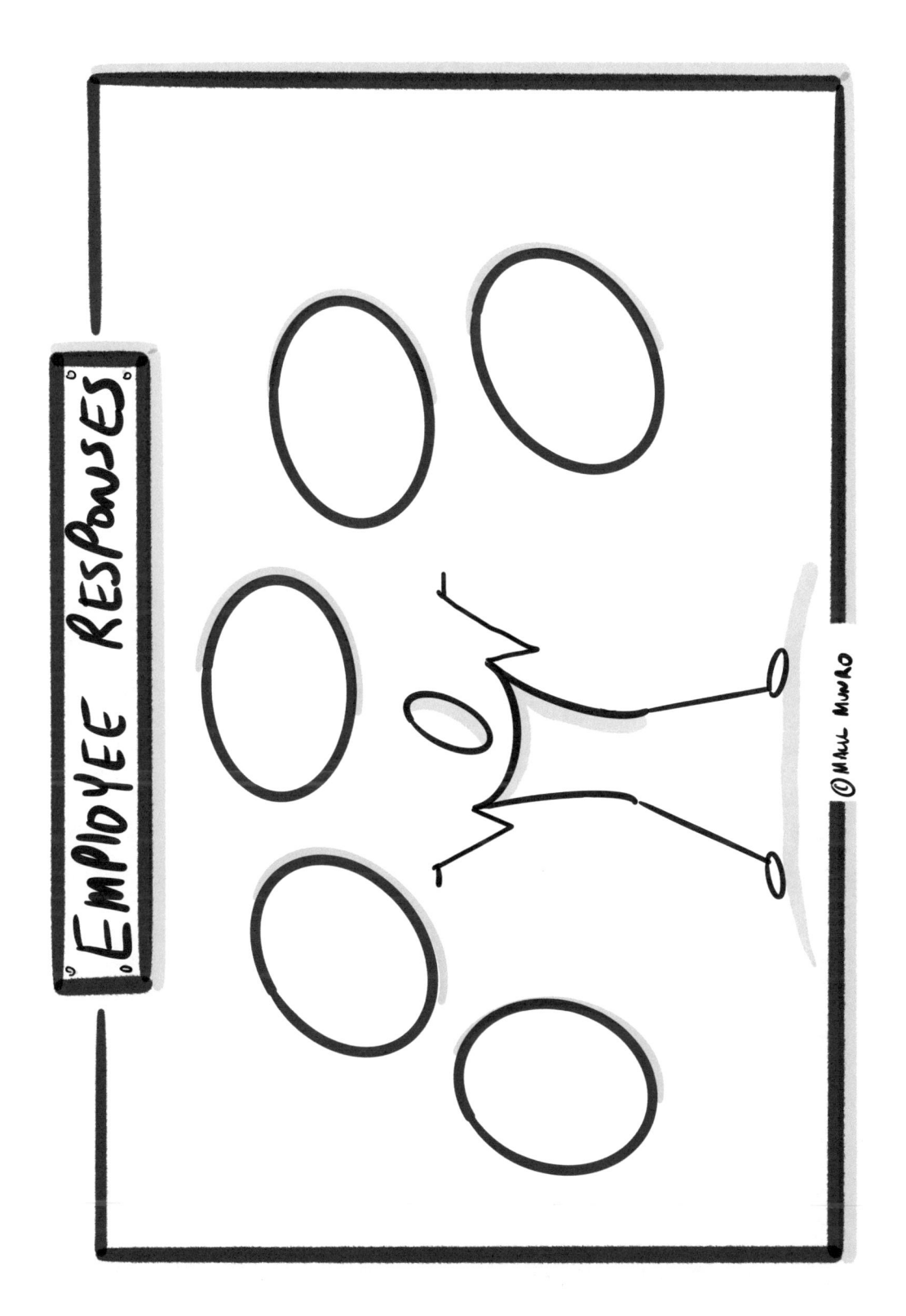

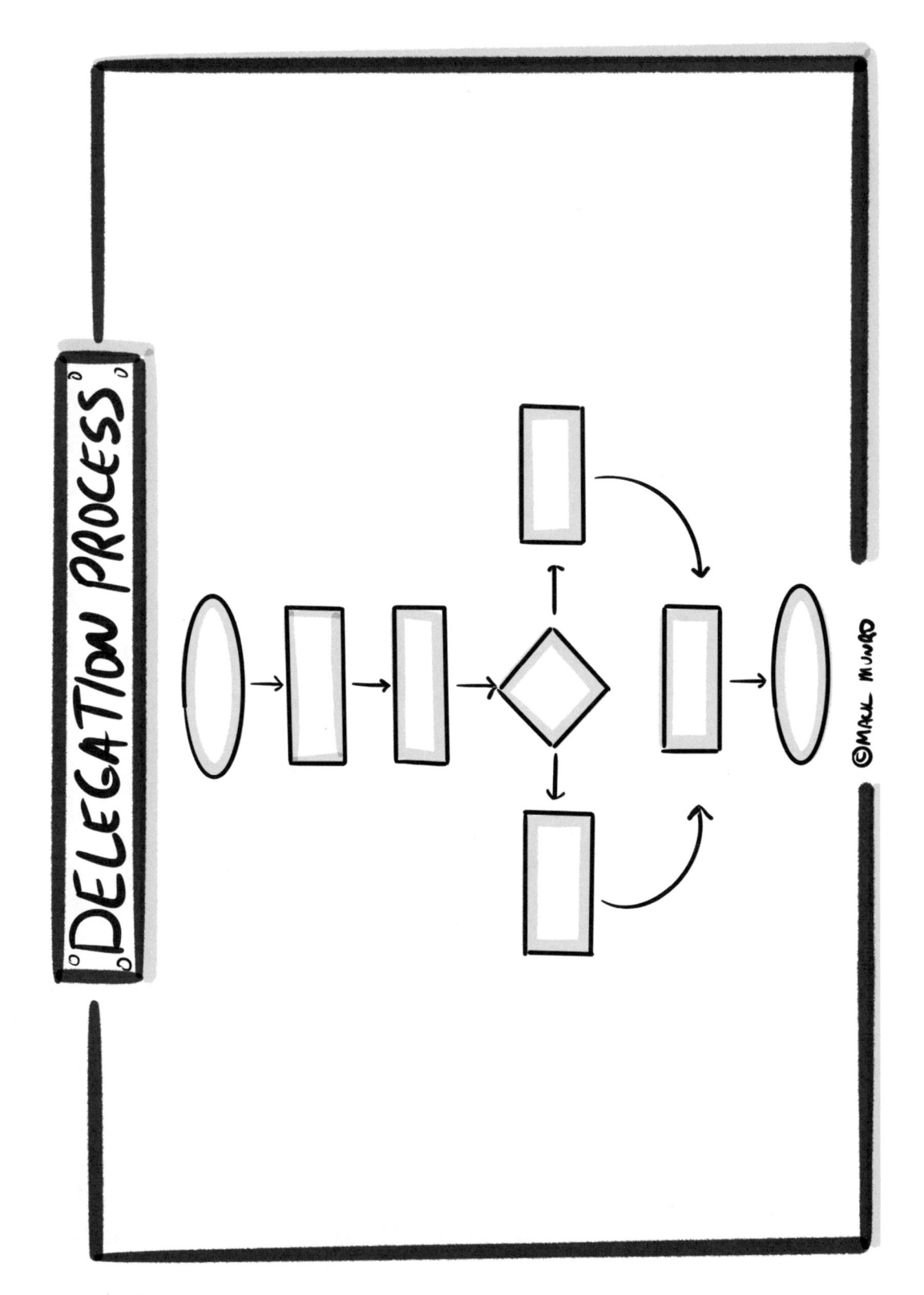

DELEGATION PROCESS

Delegation Worksheet

Pick a task that you should delegate. Remember, you're freeing up some room in your schedule to grow professionally. This is giving one of your direct reports the same opportunity.

1. Task: _____

2. Degree of urgency: High Med Low

3. Degree of importance: High Med Low

4. Outcomes required:
   -
   -
   -

5. Choice of most competent person: _____
   Why?

6. Choice of the person for whom it could be developmental: _____
   Why?
   - Does s/he have the basic skill set to produce the outcomes required?
   - What kind of coaching/support would be needed? (Do I have the time to provide it?)

7. The right person for this assignment is: _____

8. I will hold the delegation meeting on: _____

TEAM BUILDING

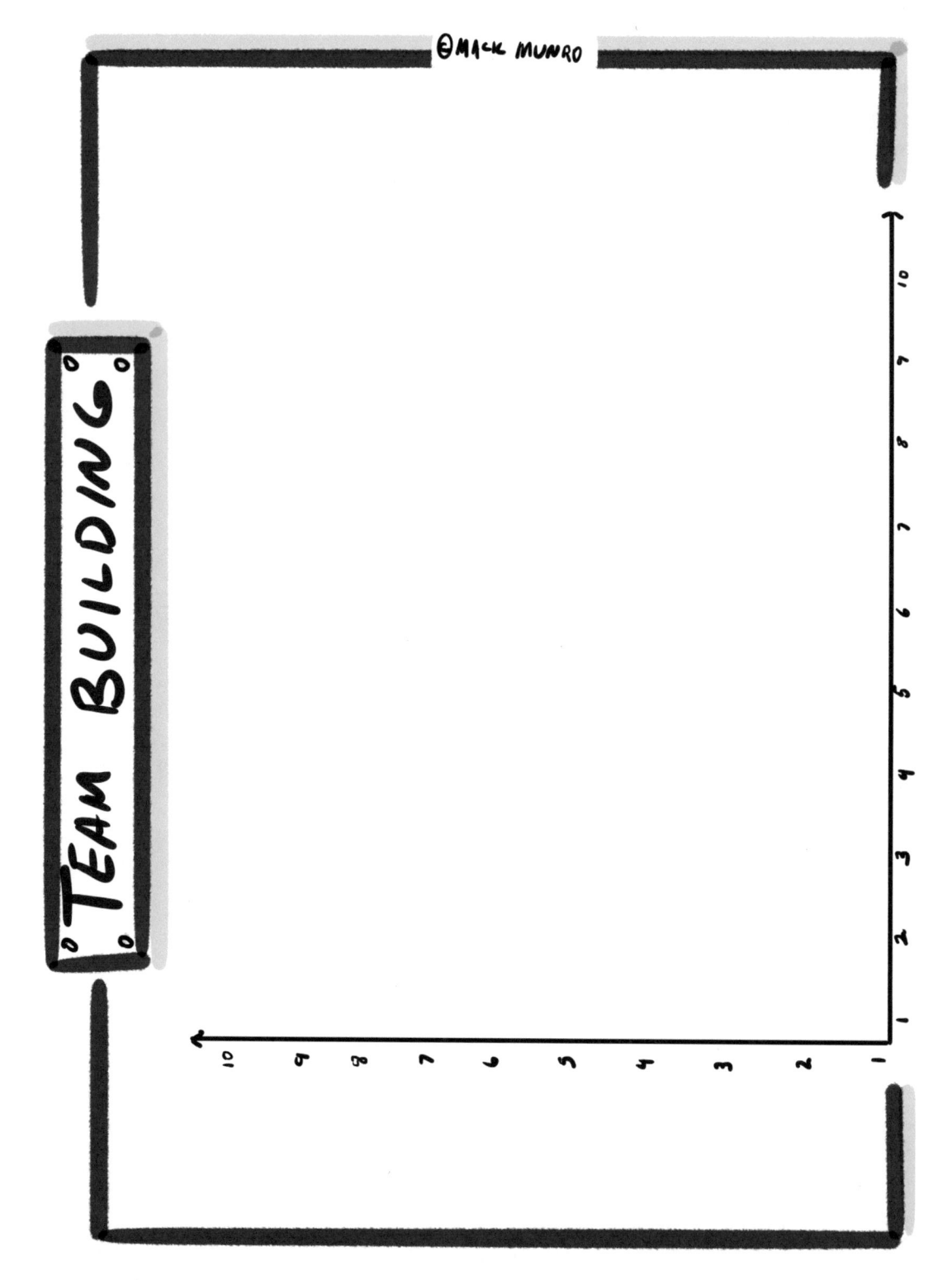

©MACK MUNRO

"Skill" Indicators

	Indicators	Team Member Initials ----->							
4	Highly skilled								
3	Moderate skill								
2	Low skill								
1	New to the to the task or to the organization								

"Will" Indicators

	Indicators	Team Member Initials ----->							
1	Totally and completely absent from participating. Present in body, but not at all there.								
2	Perceived as being very passive and uninvolved in team discussions and decisions.								
3	Seen as rarely participating or openly voicing opinions.								
4	Seen as seldom participating or openly voicing opinions, only happens when it's important to them or their department.								
5	Viewed as generally low key; occasionally will interact with others on process and discussions with strong prompting.								
6	Viewed as somewhat low key; will interact with others on process and discussions with some encouragement.								
7	Seen as actively involved in team discussions and process. Readily voices opinions and ideas.								
8	Seen as highly involved in team discussions and process. Frequently voices opinions and ideas.								
9	Perceived as overly assertive or dominant in team interactions.								
10	A complete control freak. Will dominate every aspect of a team meeting or interaction.								

"Focus" Indicators

	Indicators	Team Member Initials-----→								
1	The task is most important - above anything else. Prefer to do everything myself. I don't need anyone else.									
2	Dedicated to the task. Mission is critical. Outright unfriendly towards anyone else.									
3	Dedicated to the task. Progress must be constant. People, if involved, come second to the task.									
4	Focused on the task. Consistent performance on the task. People are relied upon only when needed.									
5	Focused on the task. Average performance on the task. People are relied upon only when necessary.									
6	Viewed as being neither particularly interested or uninterested in the task. Neither friendly or unfriendly with fellow team members.									
7	Dedicated to and focused on the task. Social and relationship-oriented with other team members. Genuine concern for both.									
8	Somewhat involved in the task. Relationships often outweigh task accomplishments.									
9	Perceived as distracted by the task. Relationships usually outweigh task accomplishments.									
10	Perceived as completely detached from the task. Team involvement is completely focused on relationships.									

TO DO LIST

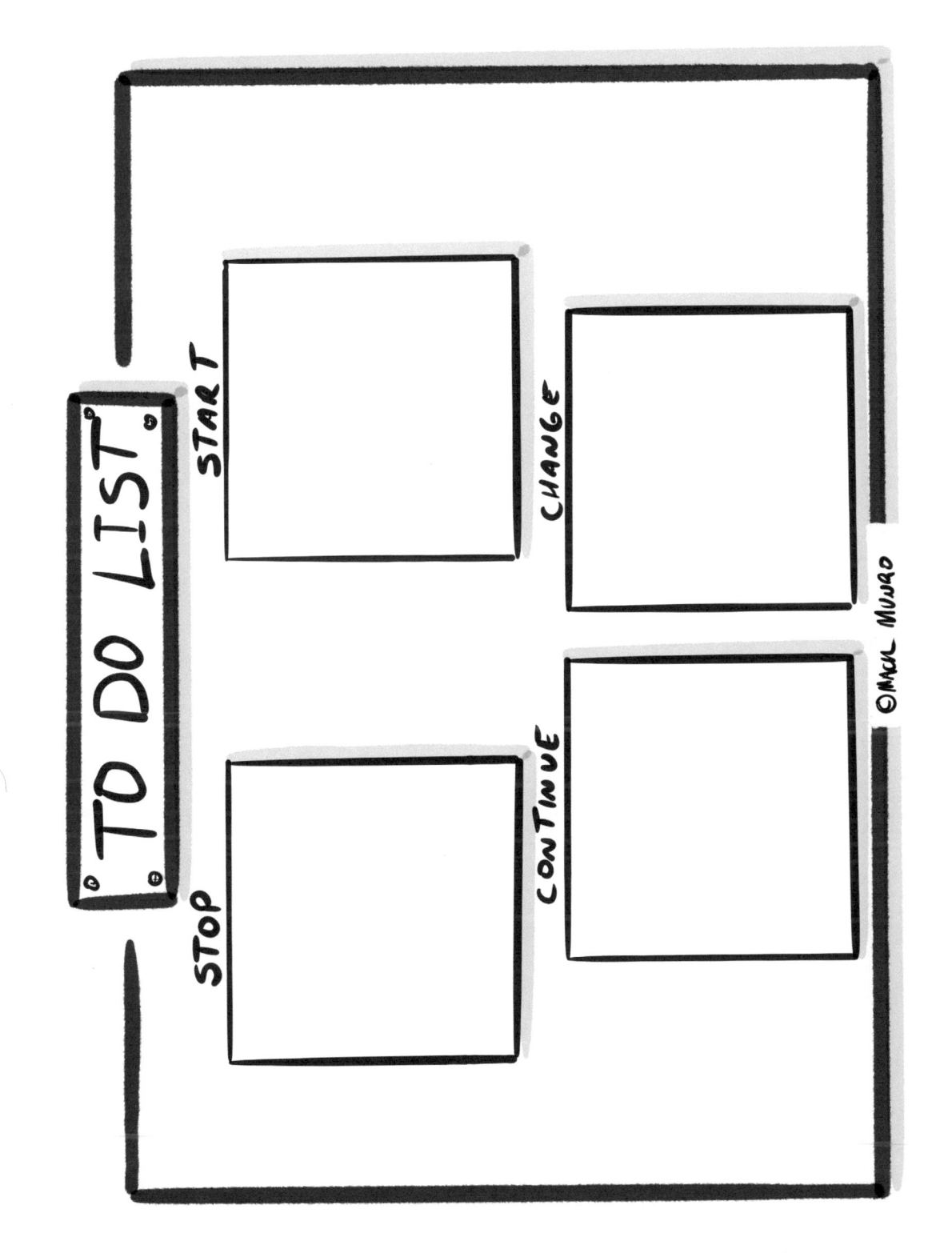

- START
- STOP
- CHANGE
- CONTINUE

THE ART OF BEING A GREAT BOSS

Notes

Session 9

Engaging Employees

Engaging Employees is designed to give you tools and techniques to develop a culture of motivation and engagement.

70 | **THE ART OF BEING A GREAT BOSS**

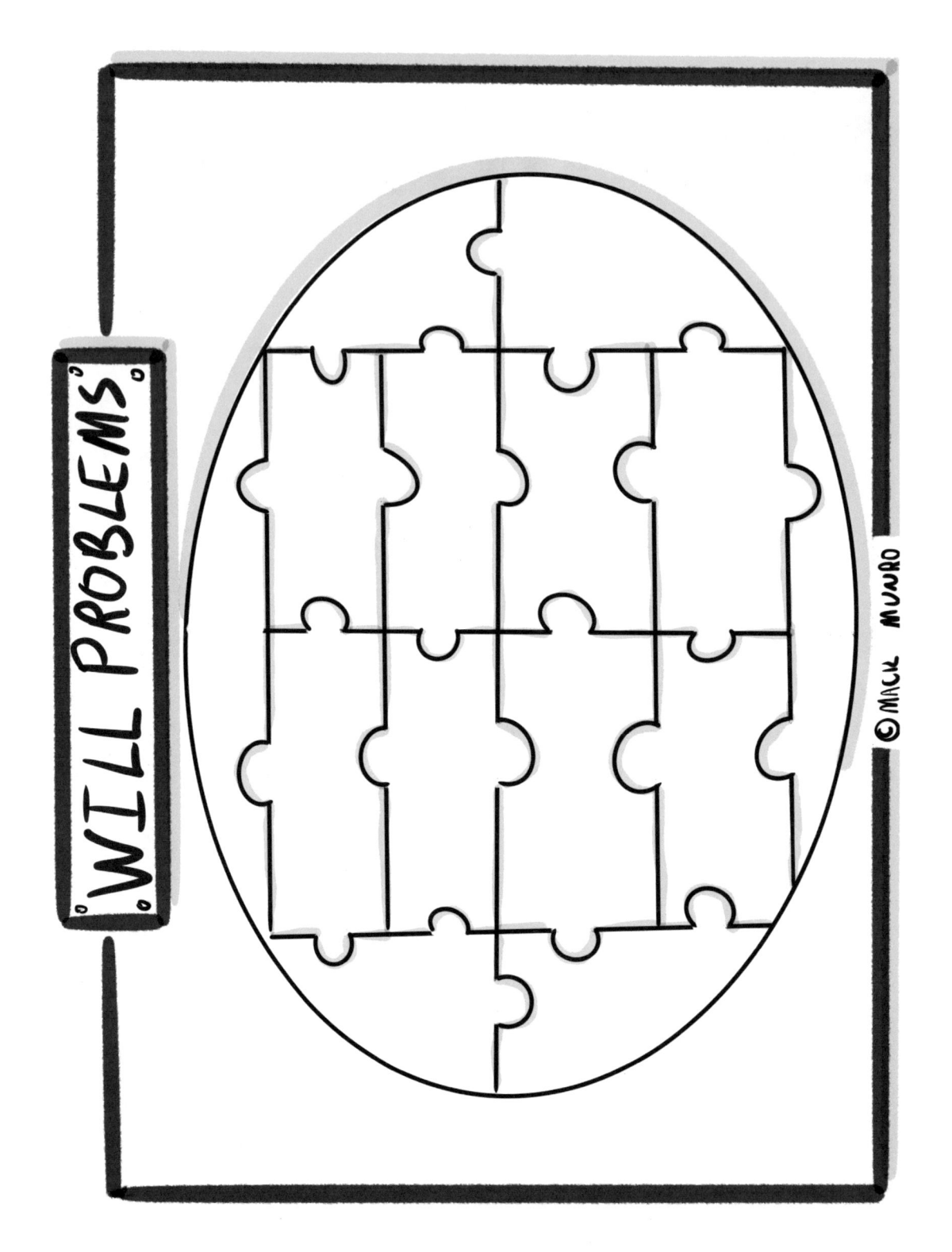

THE ART OF BEING A GREAT BOSS

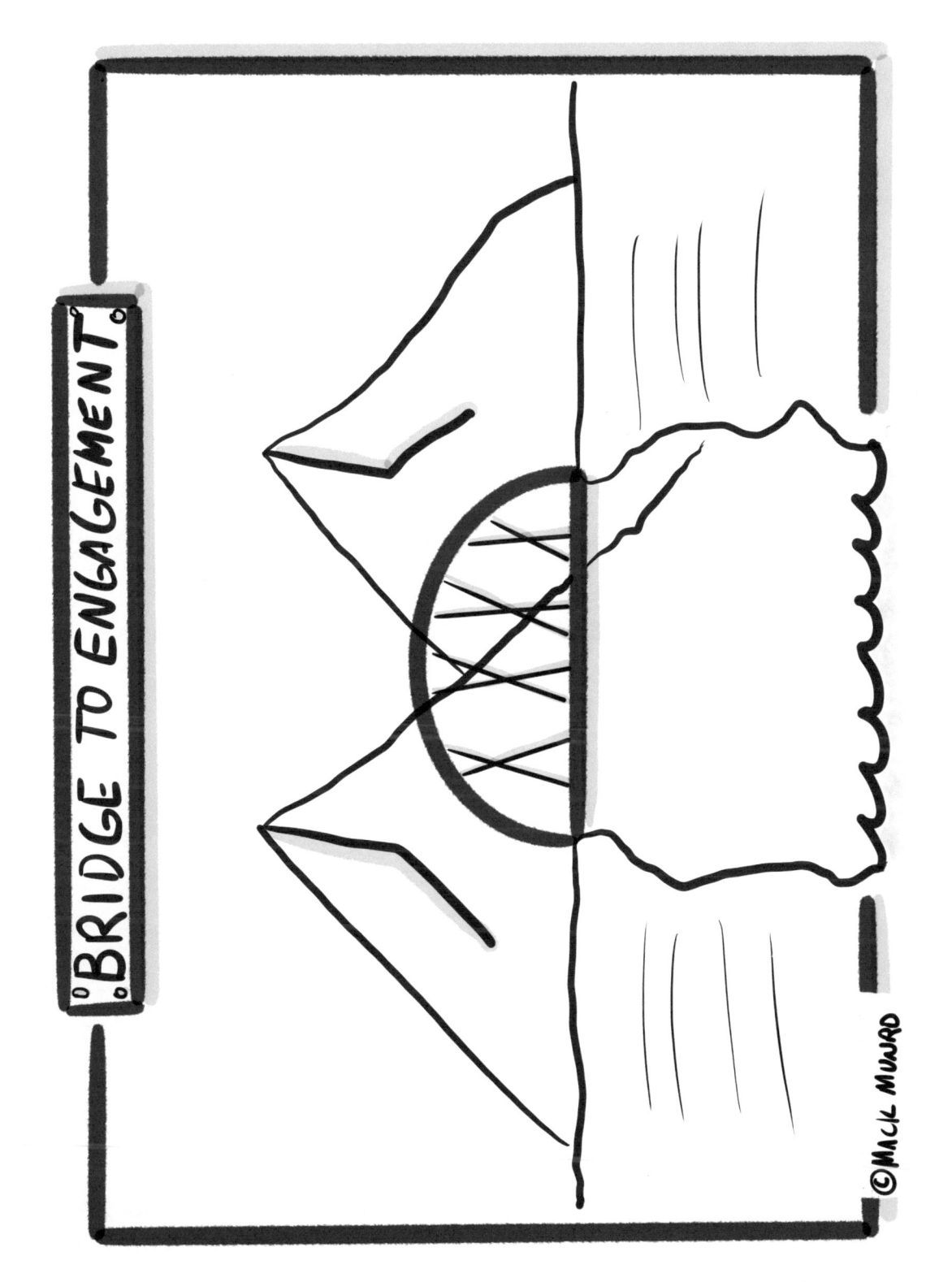

FORCE FIELD ANALYSIS

TO DO LIST

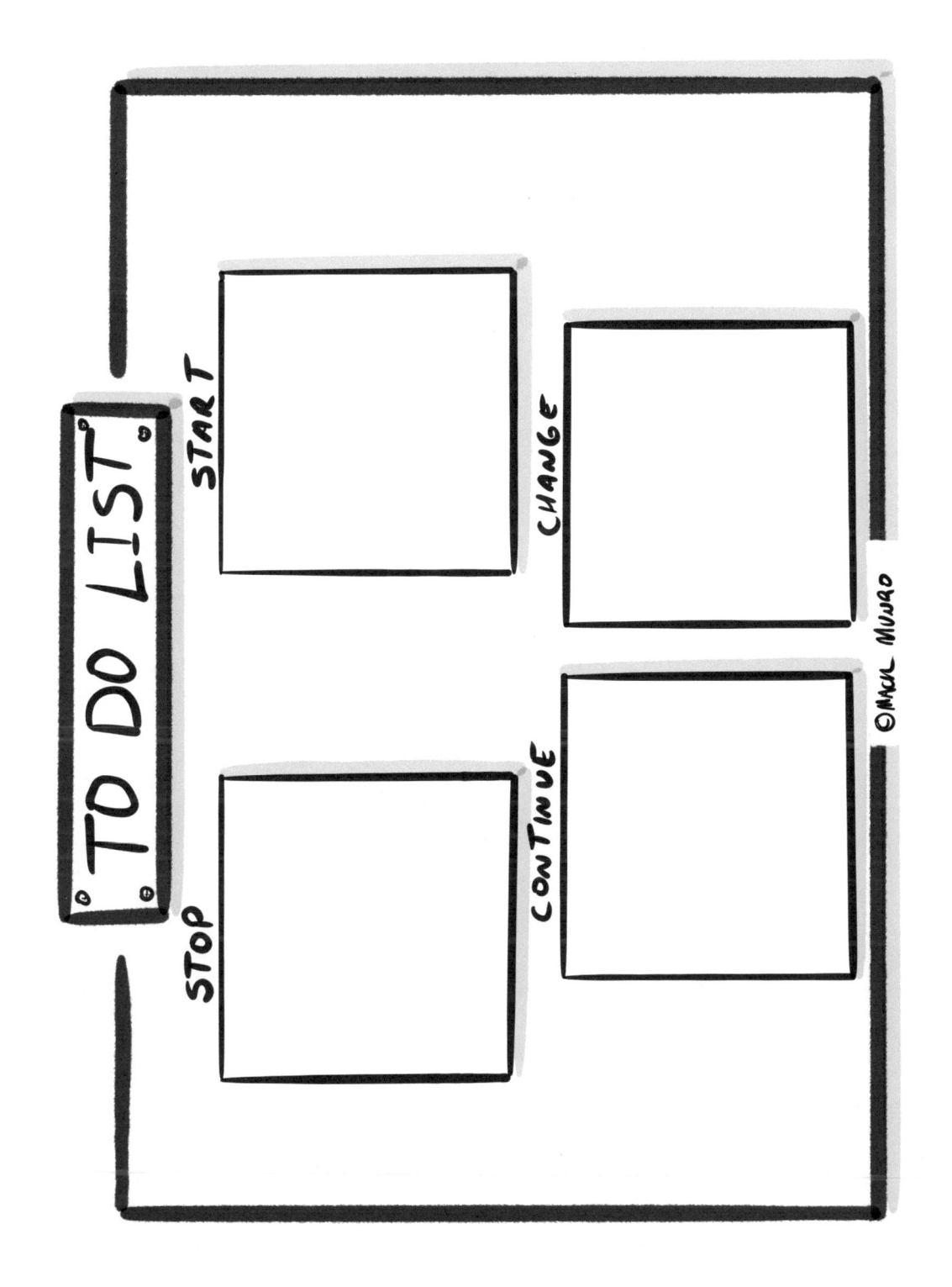

- START
- STOP
- CHANGE
- CONTINUE

THE ART OF BEING A GREAT BOSS

Notes

Session 10

Tools and Their Uses – Part 1

Improving Systems and Processes is designed to give you tools and techniques to better run your department and be seen as a critical thinker.

PROBLEM #1

STANDARDS

"I'm not as bad as the other employees."

"I work harder than anyone else."

Remedy: _____

THE ART OF BEING A GREAT BOSS | 77

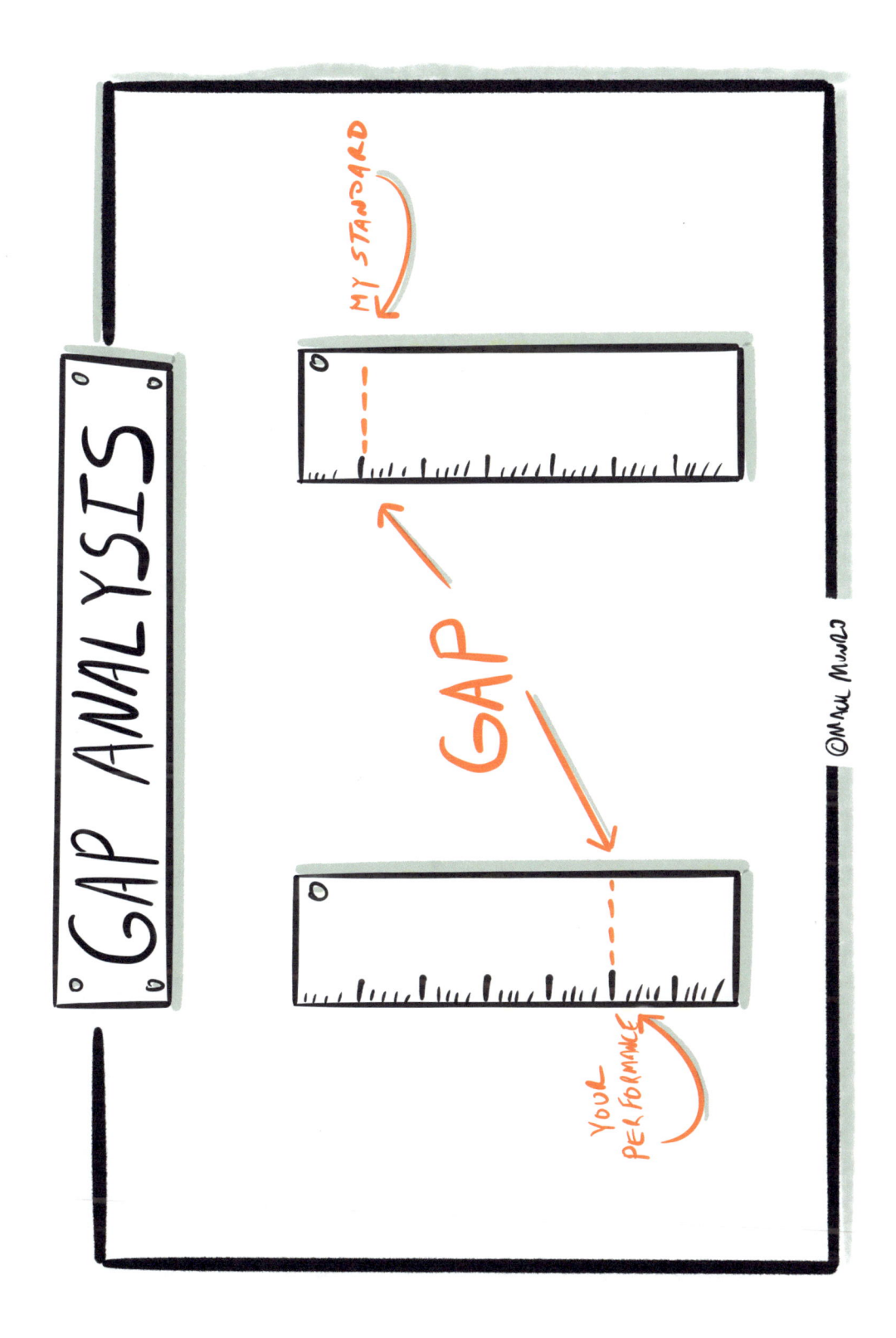

PROBLEM #2

SURFACE ISSUES

"YOU HAVE A PROBLEM HANDLING CONFLICT."

— EMPLOYEE SURVEY

REMEDY:

THE ART OF BEING A GREAT BOSS | 79

PROBLEM #3

PROCESS ISSUES

- You have a broken process
- You want to build a better process
- You want to document or teach a process

Remedy: _____

80 | THE ART OF BEING A GREAT BOSS

FLOW CHART

PROBLEM #4

WE NEED NEW IDEAS

"I HAVE NO IDEA WHAT TO DO NEXT."

"DOES ANYONE HAVE ANY SUGGESTIONS?"

REMEDY: _____

© Mack Munro

THE ART OF BEING A GREAT BOSS | 83

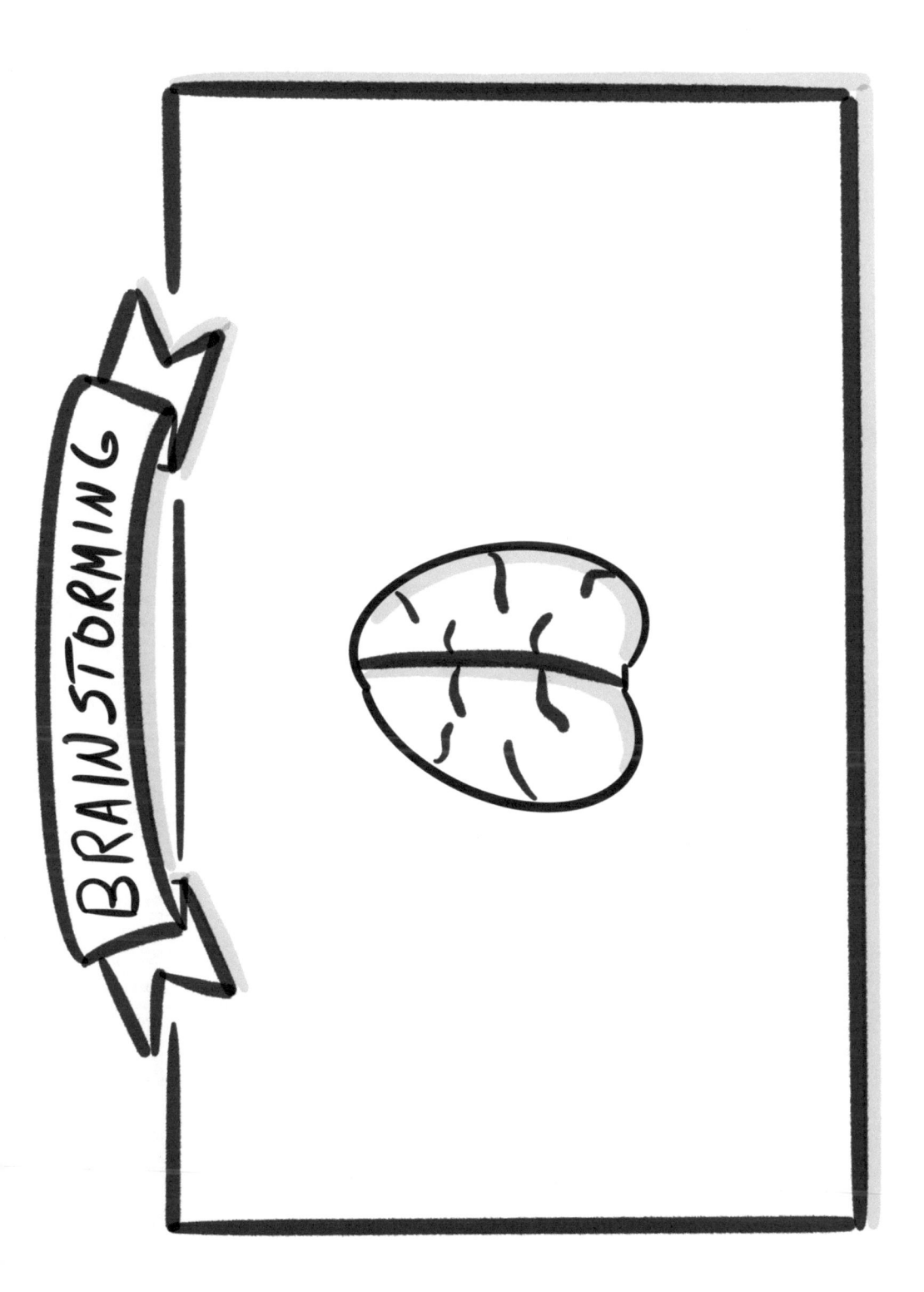

PROBLEM #5

ROOT CAUSE

"WE'VE ALWAYS DONE IT THAT WAY."

"WHOSE FAULT IS IT?"

"IT'S NOT MY PROBLEM."

"DON'T ASK WHY, JUST DO IT."

REMEDY: _____

© Jack Munro

THE ART OF BEING A GREAT BOSS | 85

Problem #6

Too Much Input

"We have too many ideas"

"How do we sort out all this data so we have something tangible?"

Remedy:

© Mack Munro

THE ART OF BEING A GREAT BOSS | 87

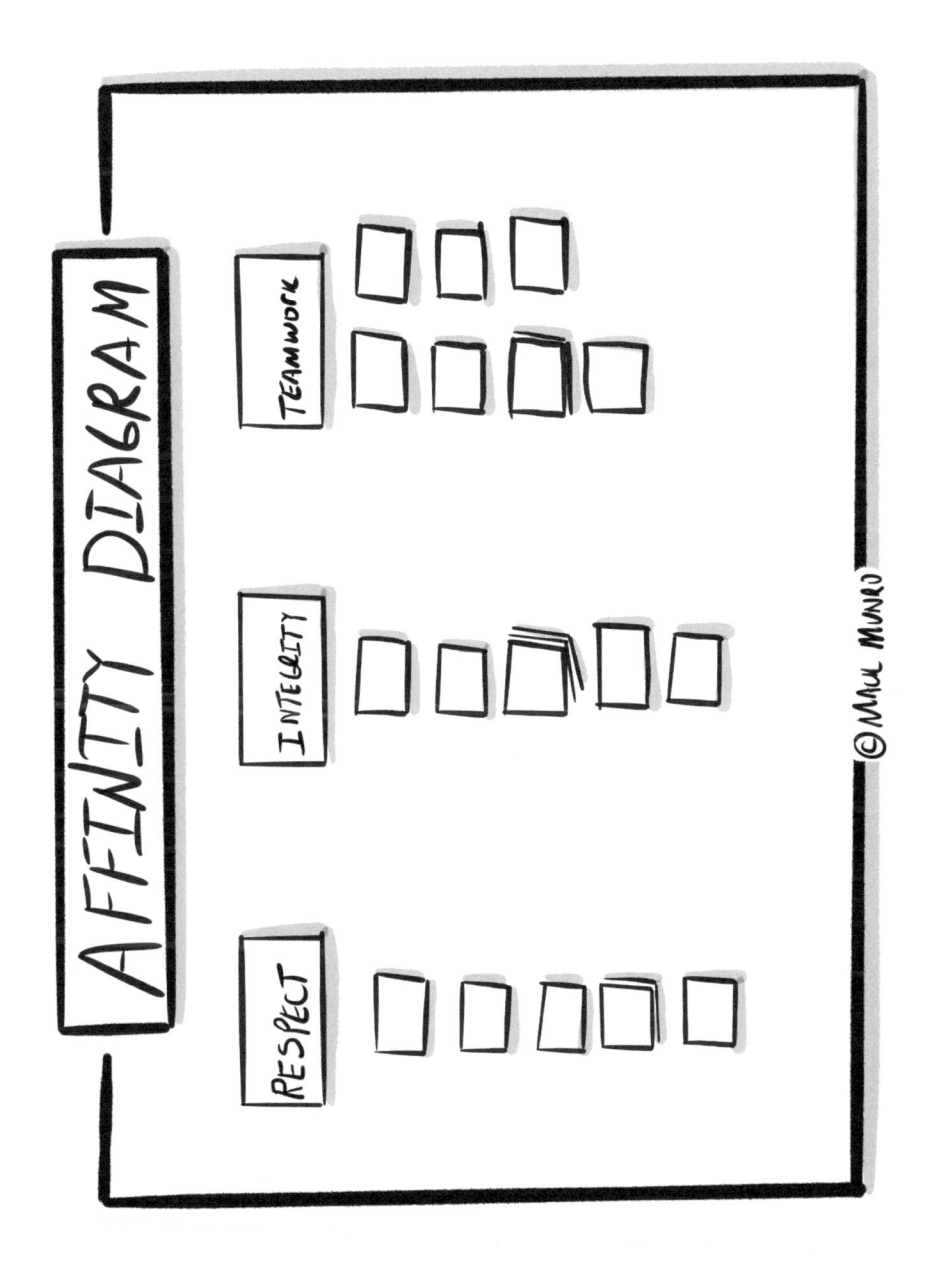

PROBLEM #7

TESTING

"Do we know if our solution is working?"

"There are so many variations! What's going on?"

REMEDY: _____

RUN CHART

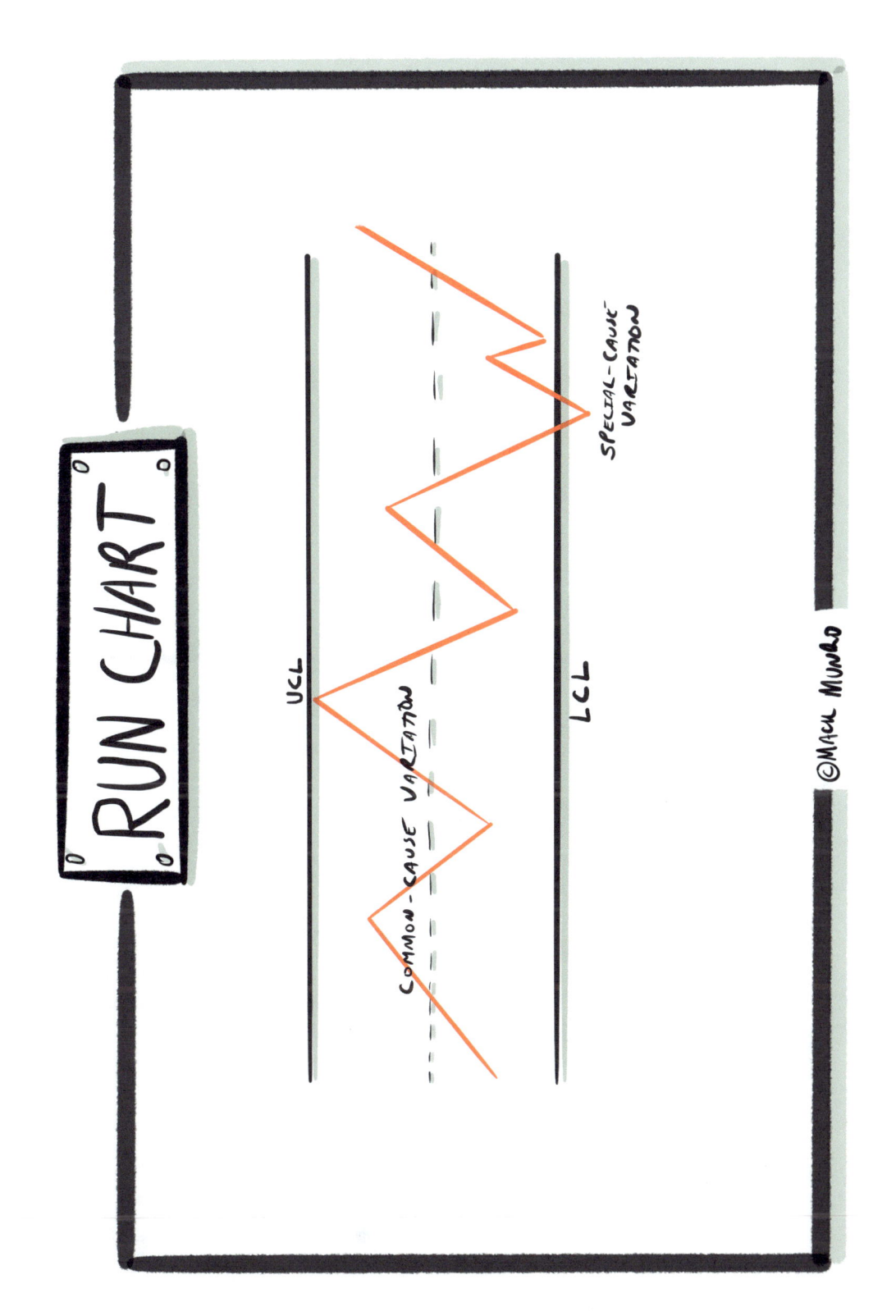

UCL

LCL

COMMON-CAUSE VARIATION

SPECIAL-CAUSE VARIATION

©MACK MUNRO

THE ART OF BEING A GREAT BOSS | 89

TO DO LIST

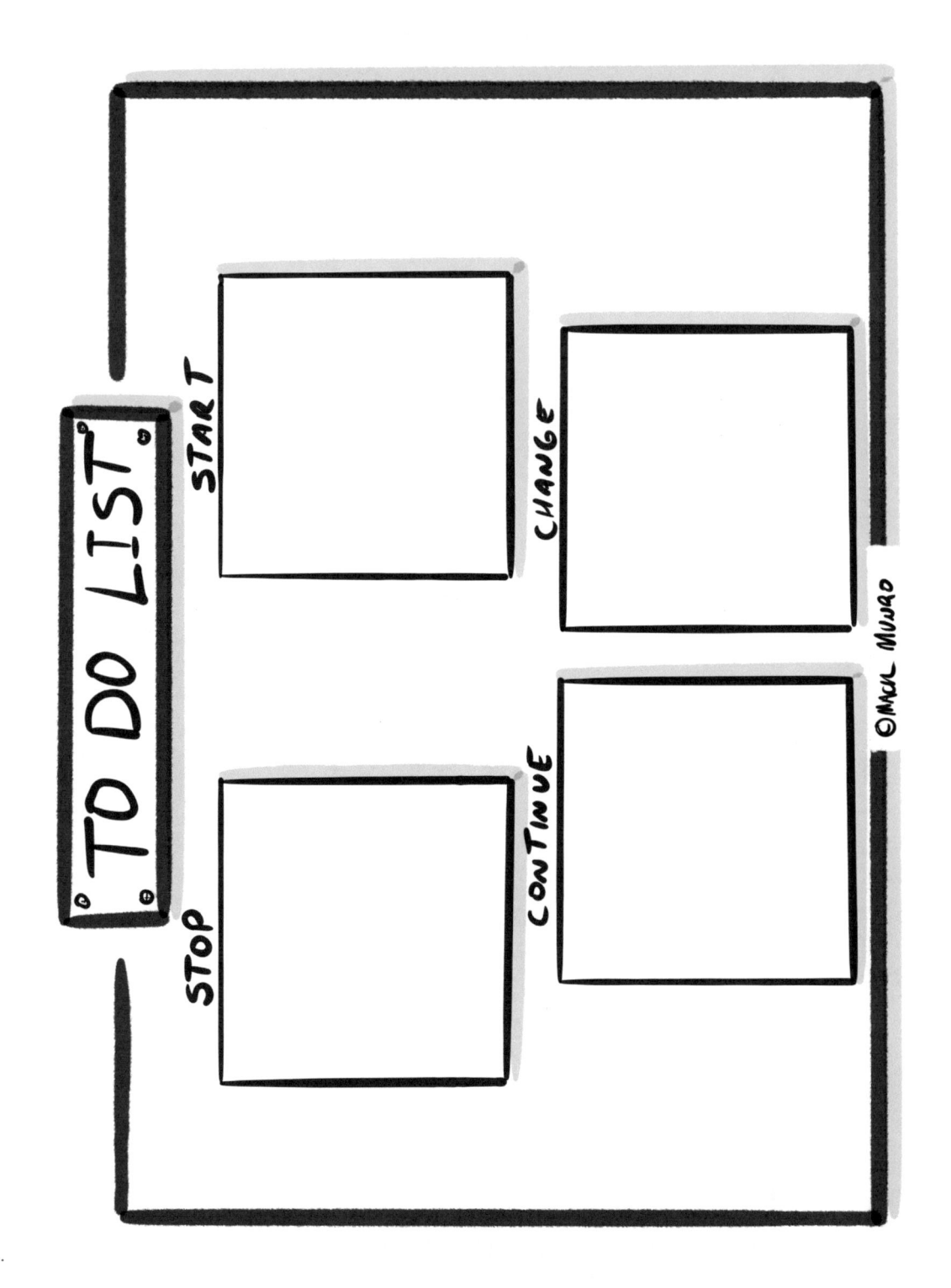

- START
- STOP
- CHANGE
- CONTINUE

©Neal Munro

Session 11

Tools and Their Uses – Part 2

Improving Systems and Processes is designed to give you tools and techniques to better run your department and be seen as a critical thinker.

PROBLEM #8

CHANGE

"WHY ARE PEOPLE FREAKING OUT OVER THIS TINY CHANGE?"

"WHY AREN'T PEOPLE TAKING THIS CHANGE SERIOUSLY?"

"WHY AREN'T PEOPLE MORE PRODUCTIVE IN THIS EXCITING NEW CHANGE?"

REMEDY:

© MACK MUNRO

92 | THE ART OF BEING A GREAT BOSS

THE ART OF BEING A GREAT BOSS | 93

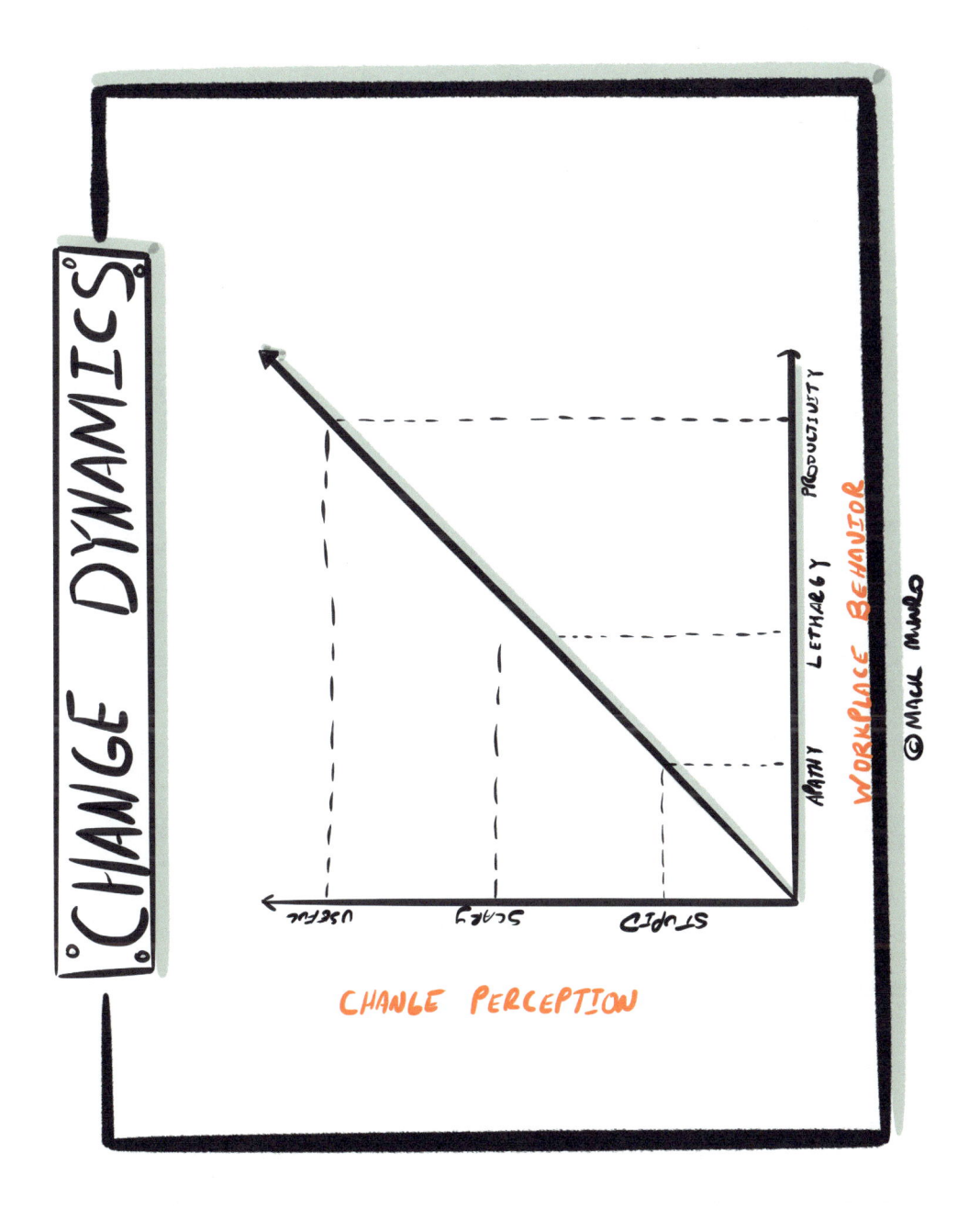

PROBLEM #9

PREDICTABILITY

"WHY DOES IT SEEM EVERYTHING IS SO PREDICTABLE?"

"I GUARANTEE THIS WILL HAPPEN AGAIN. YOU JUST WATCH!"

REMEDY: _____

© Mack Munro

Circular Causal Loop

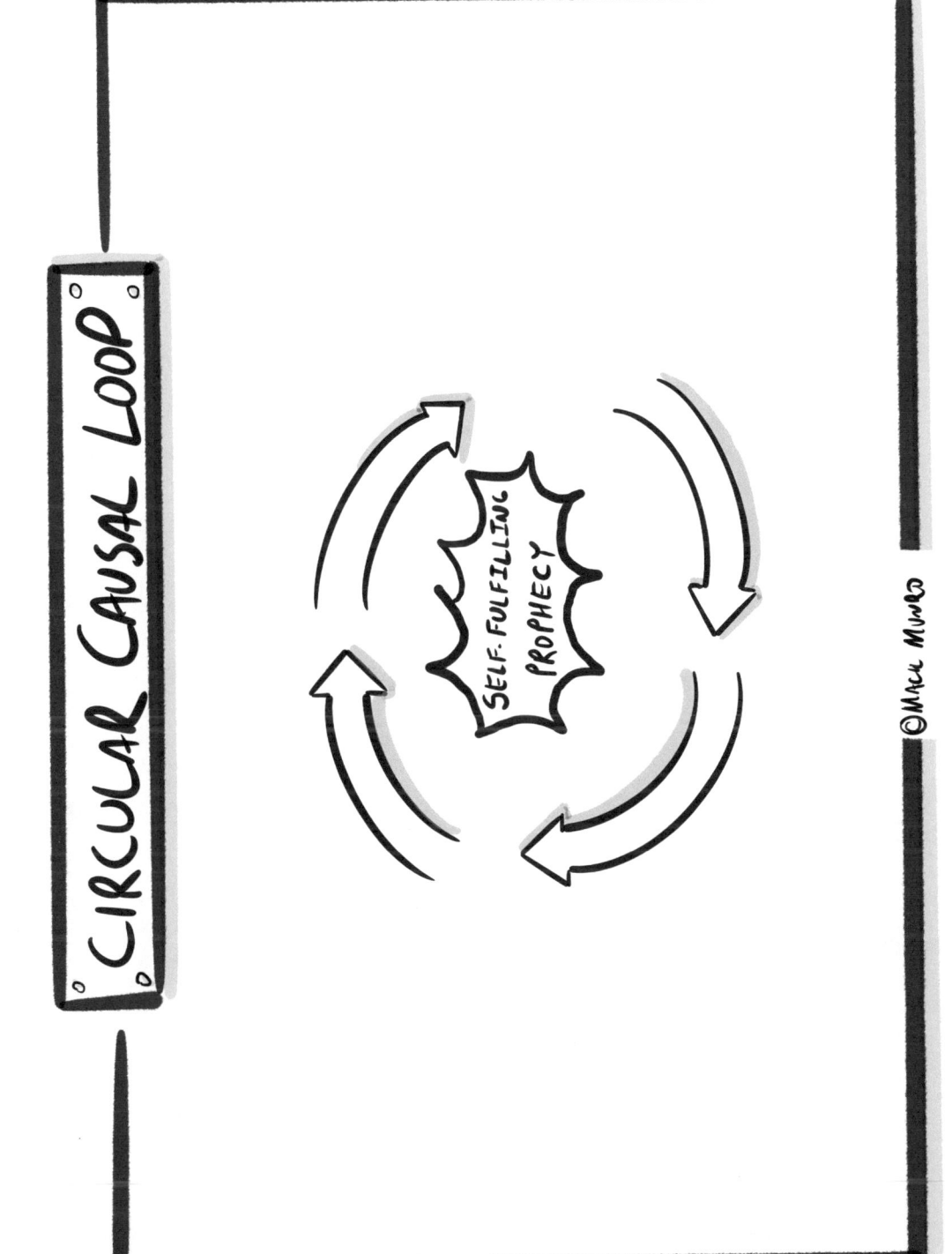

Self-Fulfilling Prophecy

THE ART OF BEING A GREAT BOSS

PROBLEM #10

EXPENSIVE SOLUTIONS

"YEAH, THIS EXPENSIVE THING SEEMS LIKE THE PERFECT SOLUTION TO THE PROBLEM."

"HELL NO! I'M NOT SPENDING THAT MUCH MONEY ON THE PROBLEM!"

REMEDY: _____

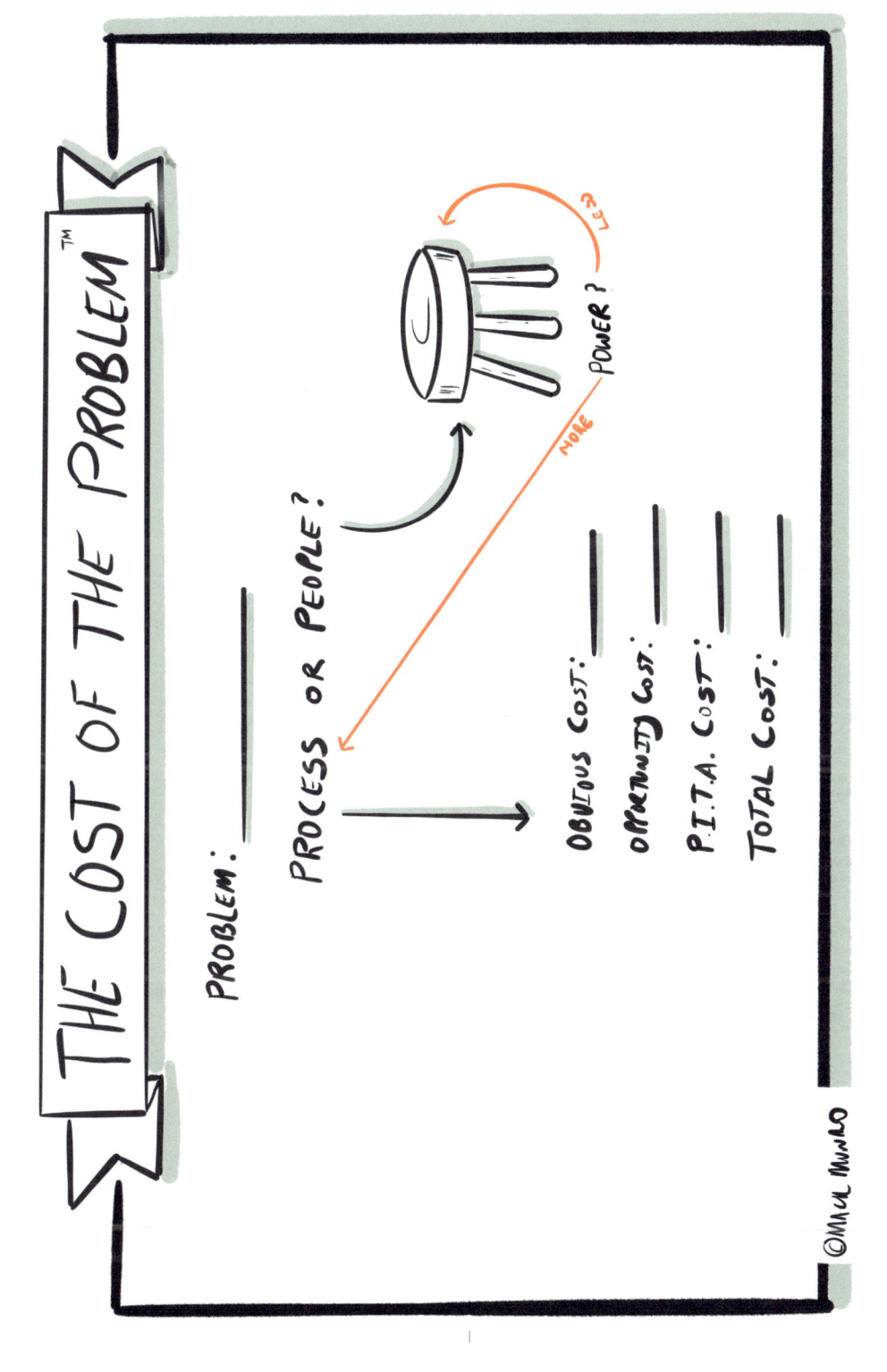

The Cost of the Problem™

Problem: _____

Process or People?

More Power? Less

- Obvious Cost: _____
- Opportunity Cost: _____
- P.I.T.A. Cost: _____
- Total Cost: _____

©Mack Munro

THE ART OF BEING A GREAT BOSS

PROBLEM #11

Will the solution work?

"This is a big deal! I hope we don't fail!"

"I think this is a great idea! I'm sure everyone else will love it."

Remedy: _____

© Jack Munro

98 | THE ART OF BEING A GREAT BOSS

WHAT WOULD HAVE TO BE TRUE?

THE PRE-MORTEM

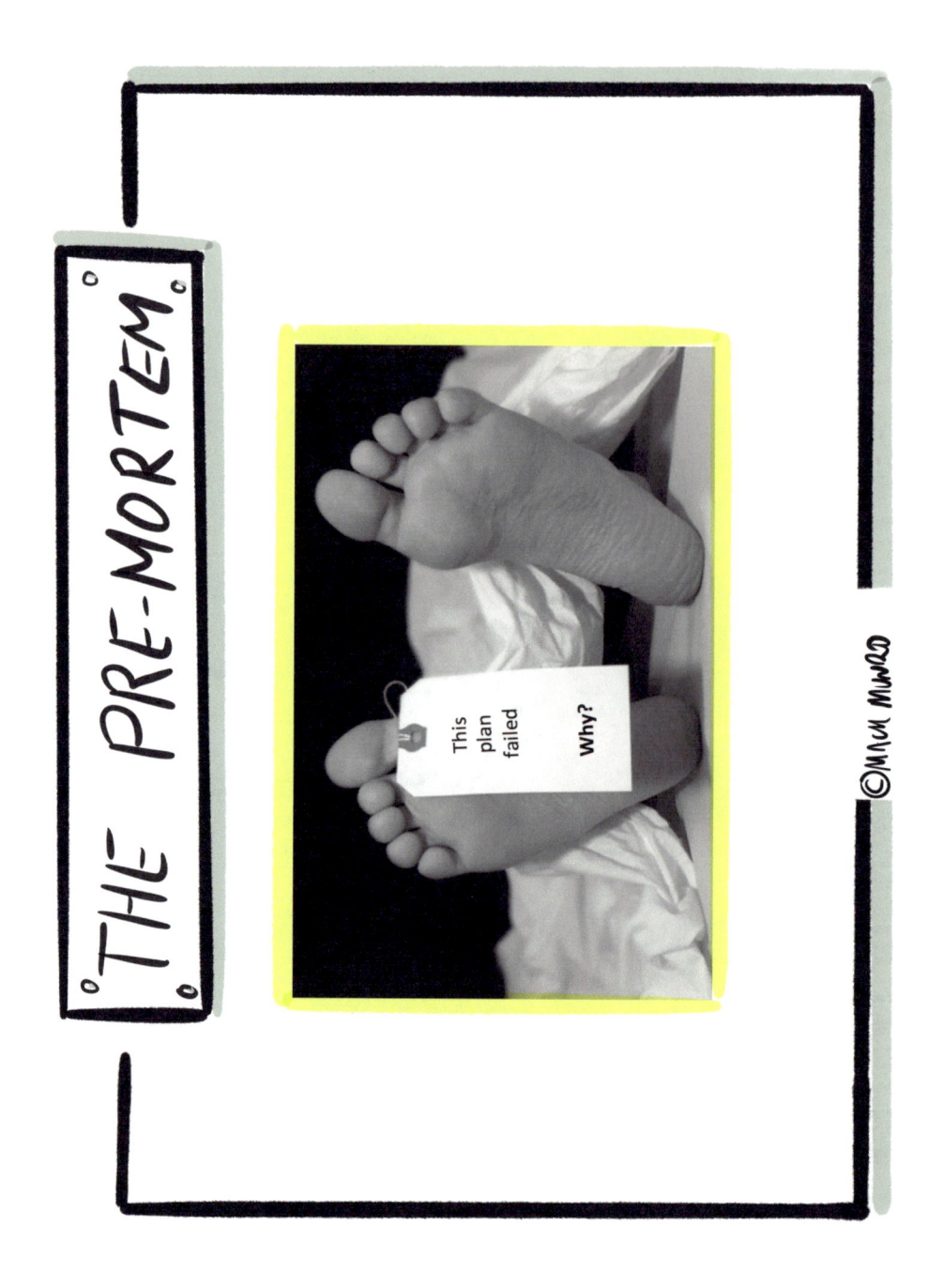

TO DO LIST

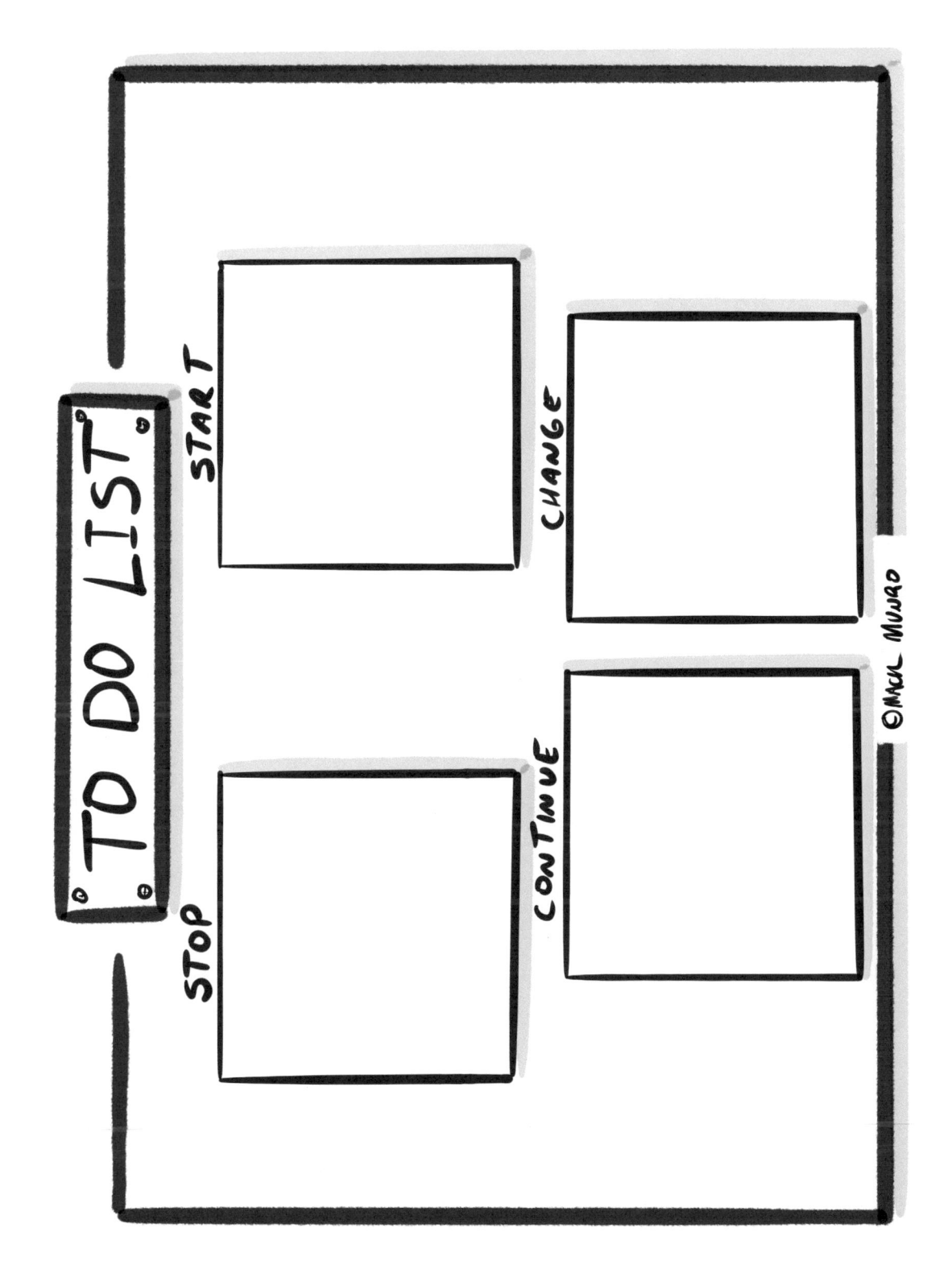

	START	CHANGE
	STOP	CONTINUE

Notes

Session 12

Your Power and Influence

Your Power and Influence is designed to give you new data regarding your own personal power and your most comfortable styles of influence.

BOSS vs. LEADER

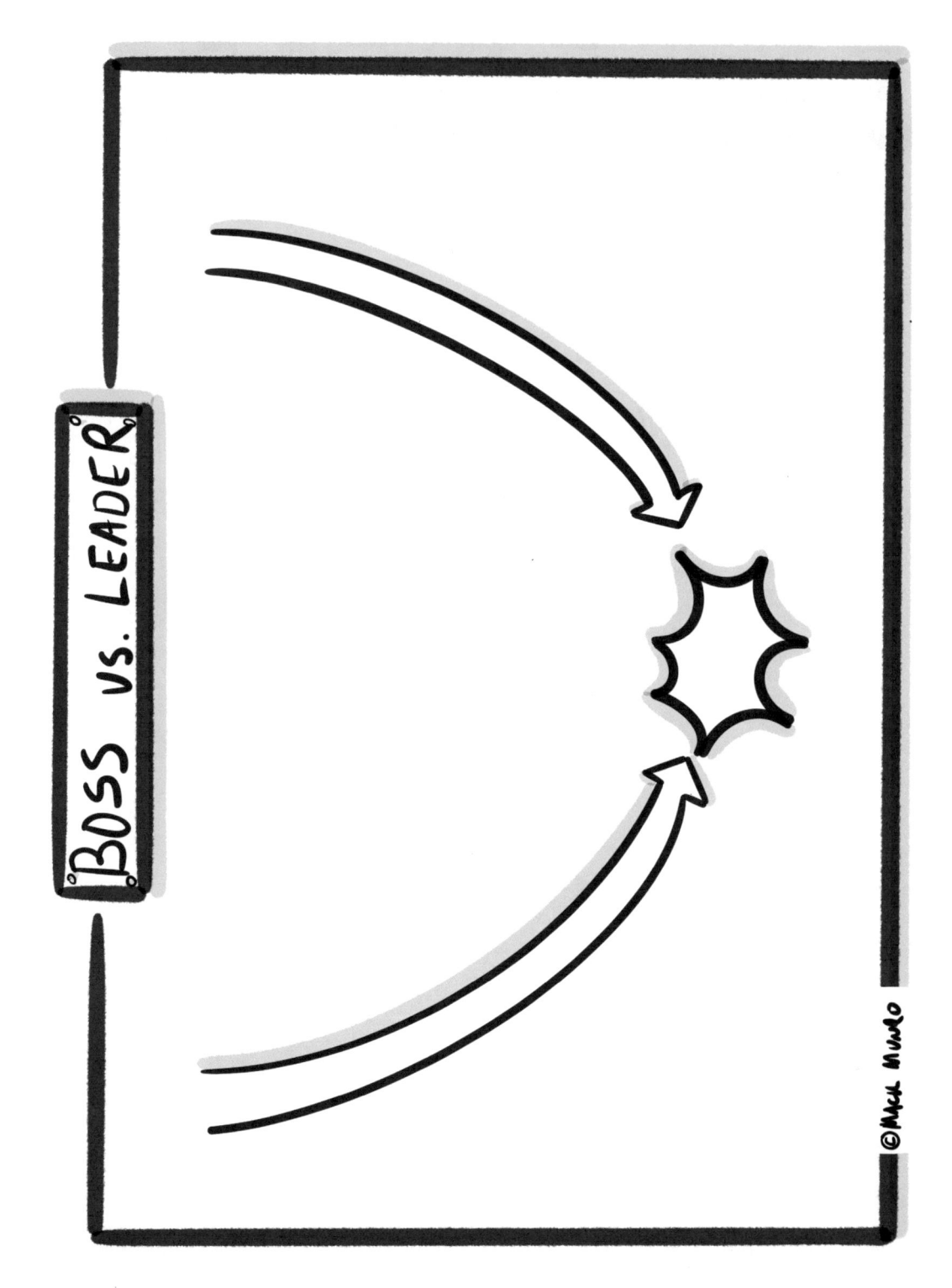

THE ART OF BEING A GREAT BOSS

SCORE:
5 - ALWAYS
4 - A LOT
3 - SOME
2 - RARELY
1 - NEVER

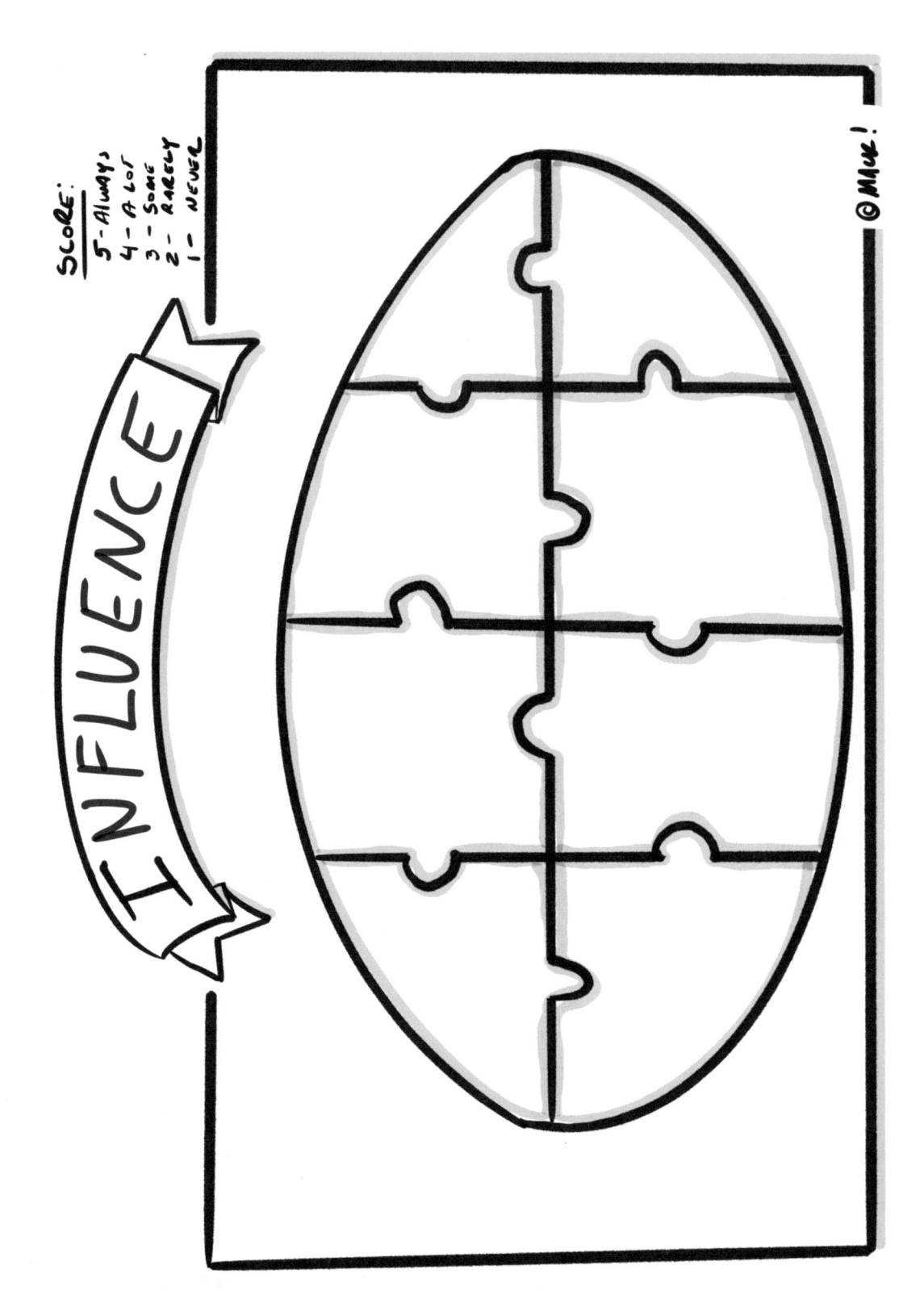

INFLUENCE

TO DO LIST

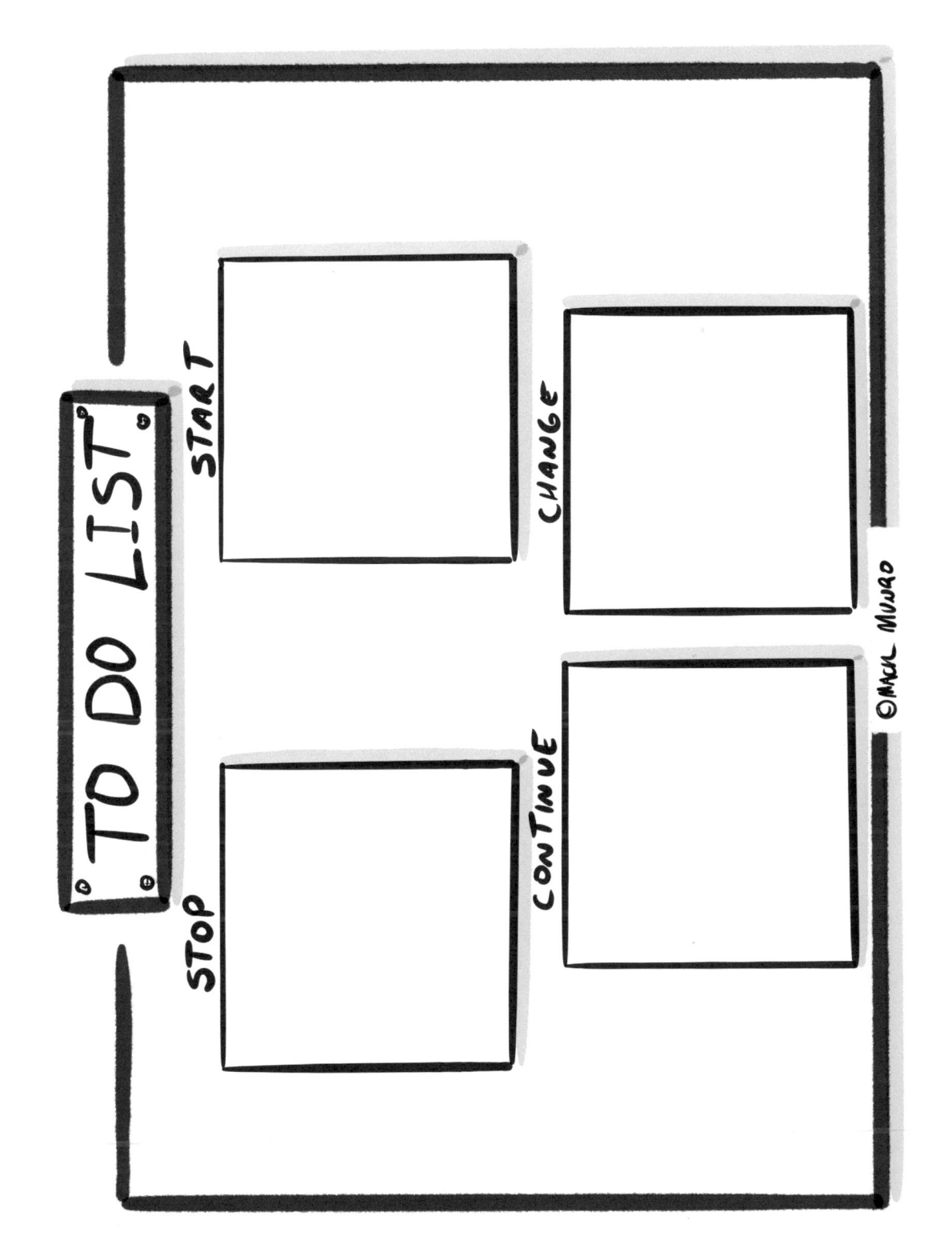

- START
- STOP
- CHANGE
- CONTINUE

©Mack Munro

THE ART OF BEING A GREAT BOSS | 107

Notes

Session 13

Navigating Organizational Politics

Navigating Organizational Politics is designed to give you tools and techniques to better leverage your power and influence to get your team seen, heard, and respected.

110 | THE ART OF BEING A GREAT BOSS

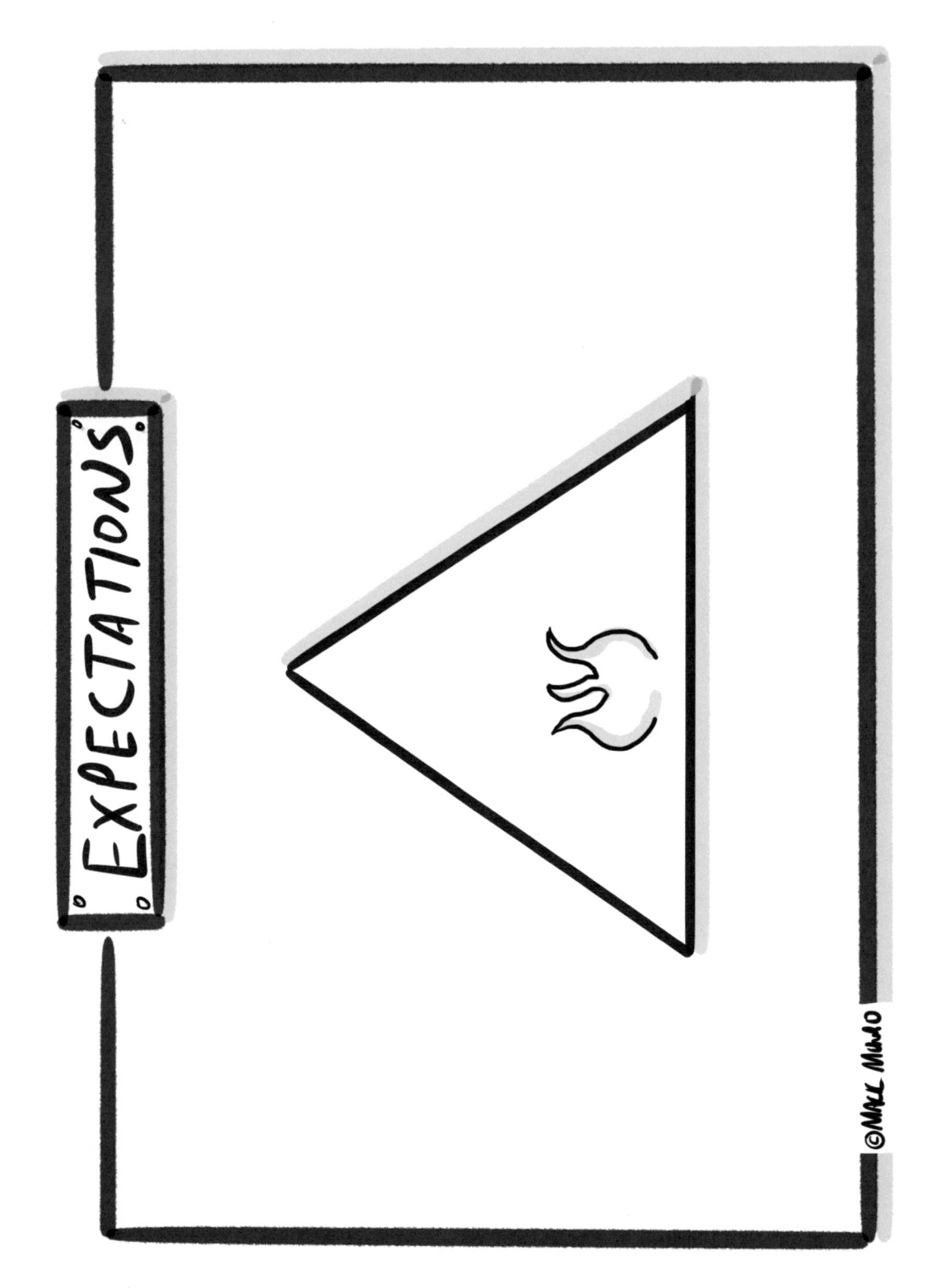

POLITICAL ATTITUDES

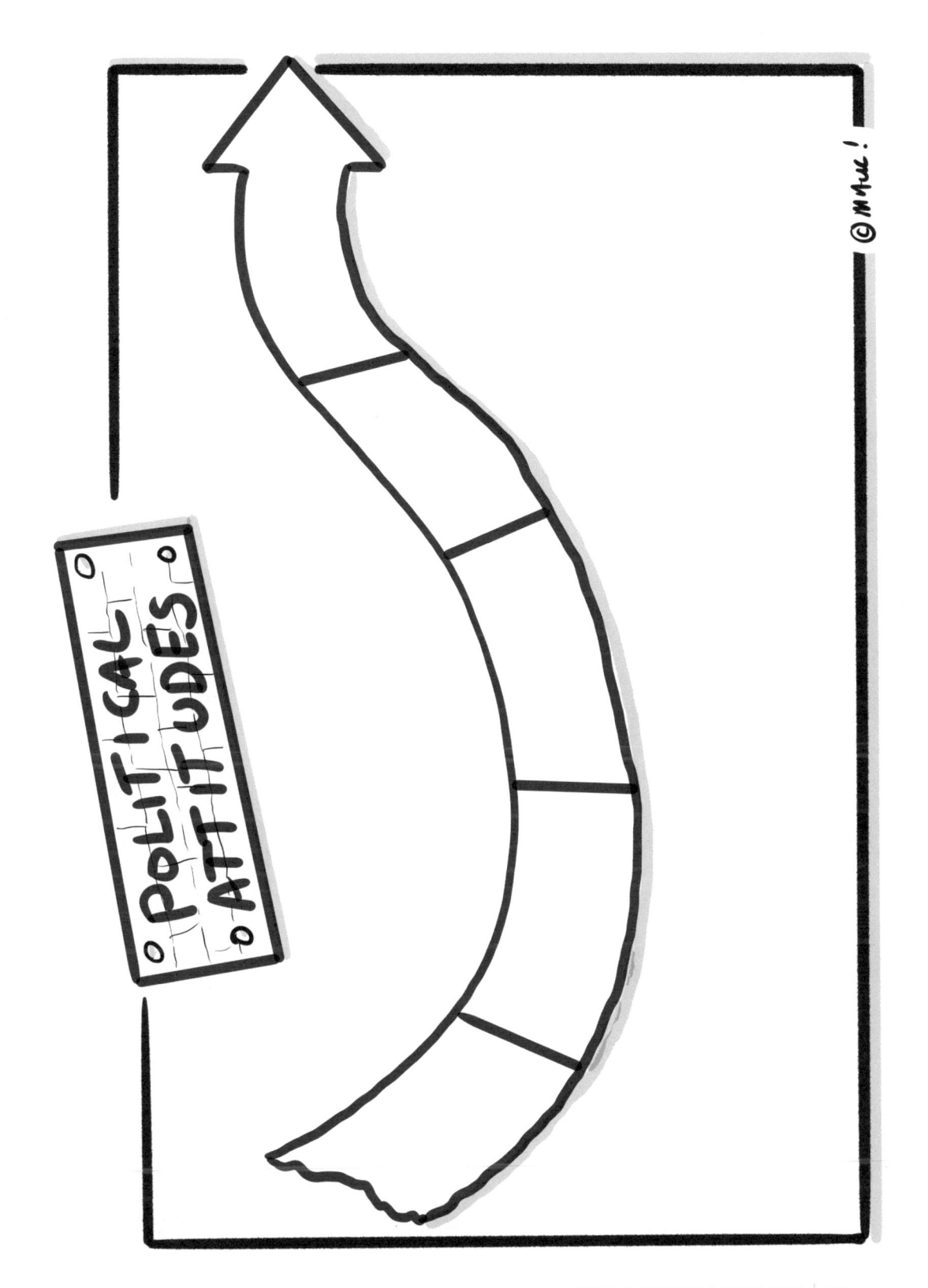

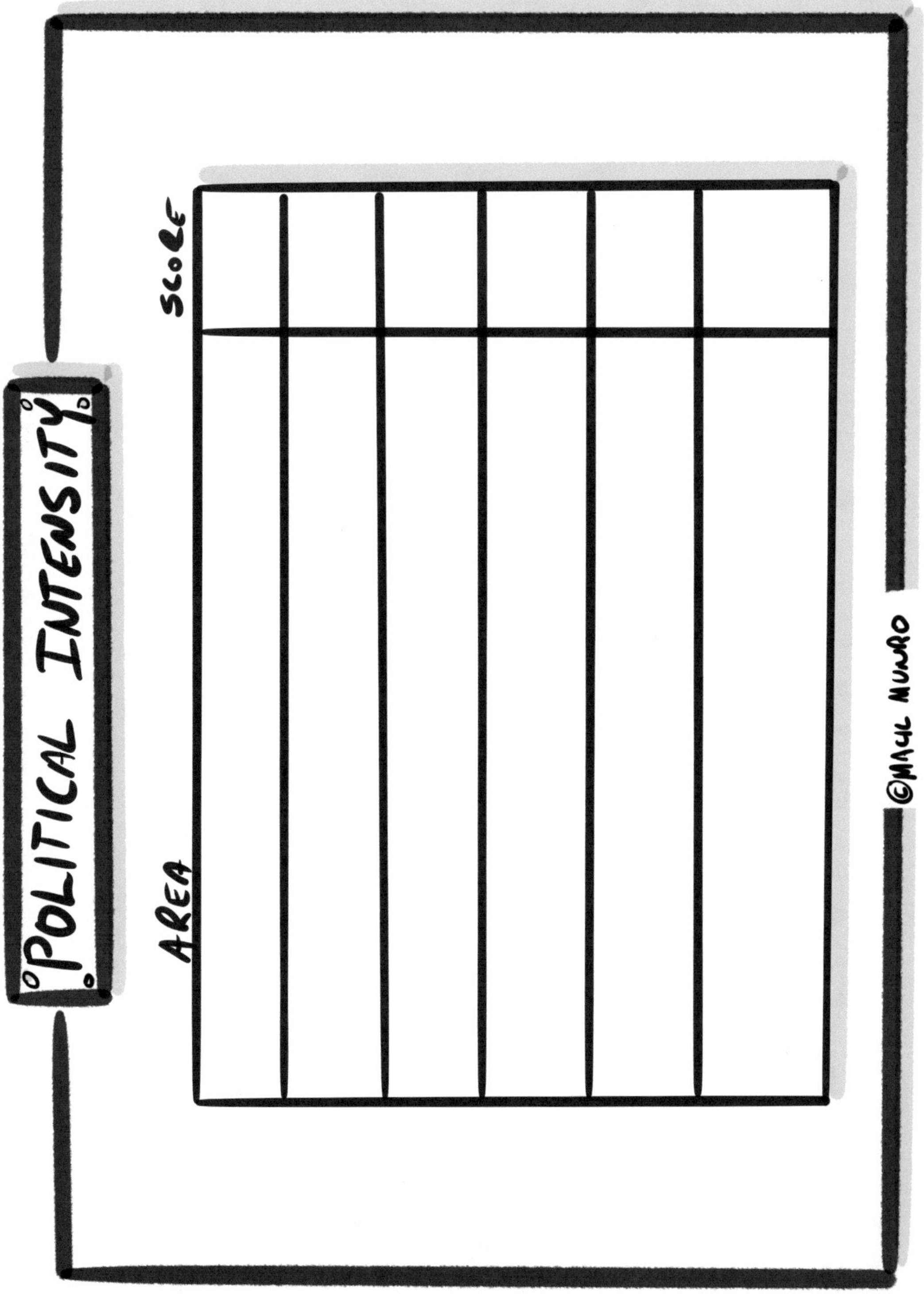
POLITICAL INTENSITY
AREA
SCORE
©MARK MUNRO

Your Goal:

Use _____ and _____ to _____ get what I for _____ me and my team to _____ !

THE ART OF BEING A GREAT BOSS

THE ART OF BEING A GREAT BOSS

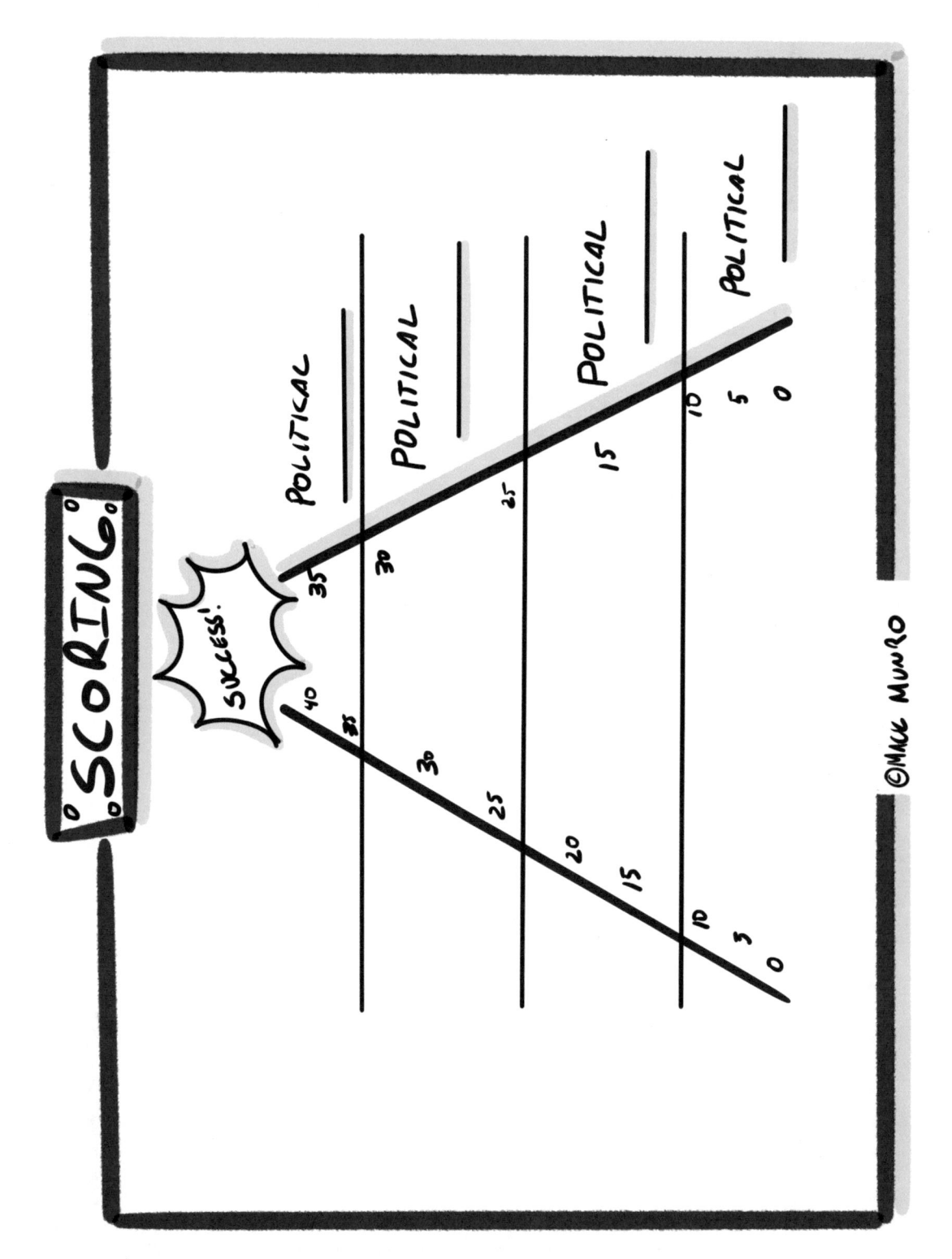

...THE GAME!

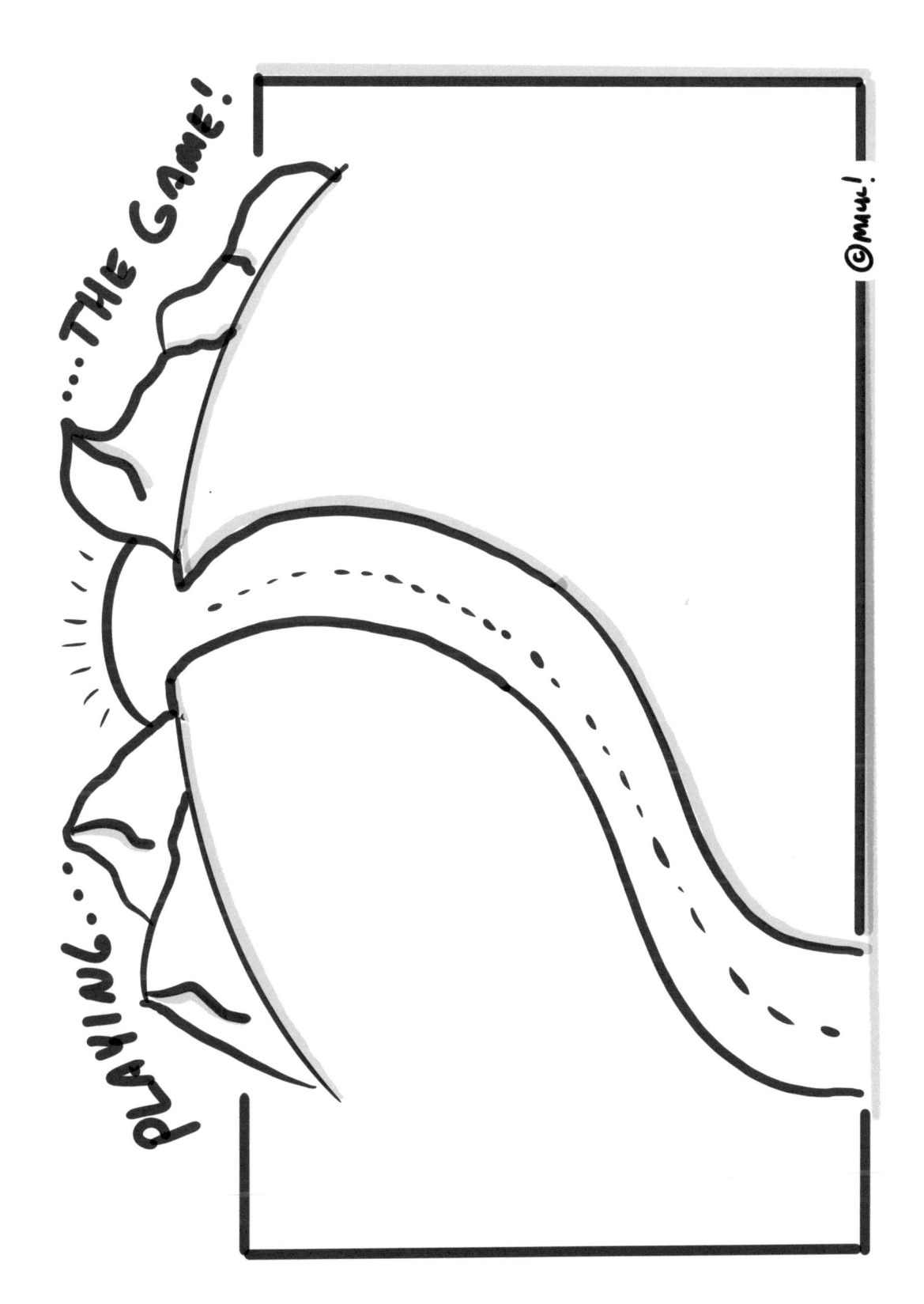

PLAYING...

TO DO LIST

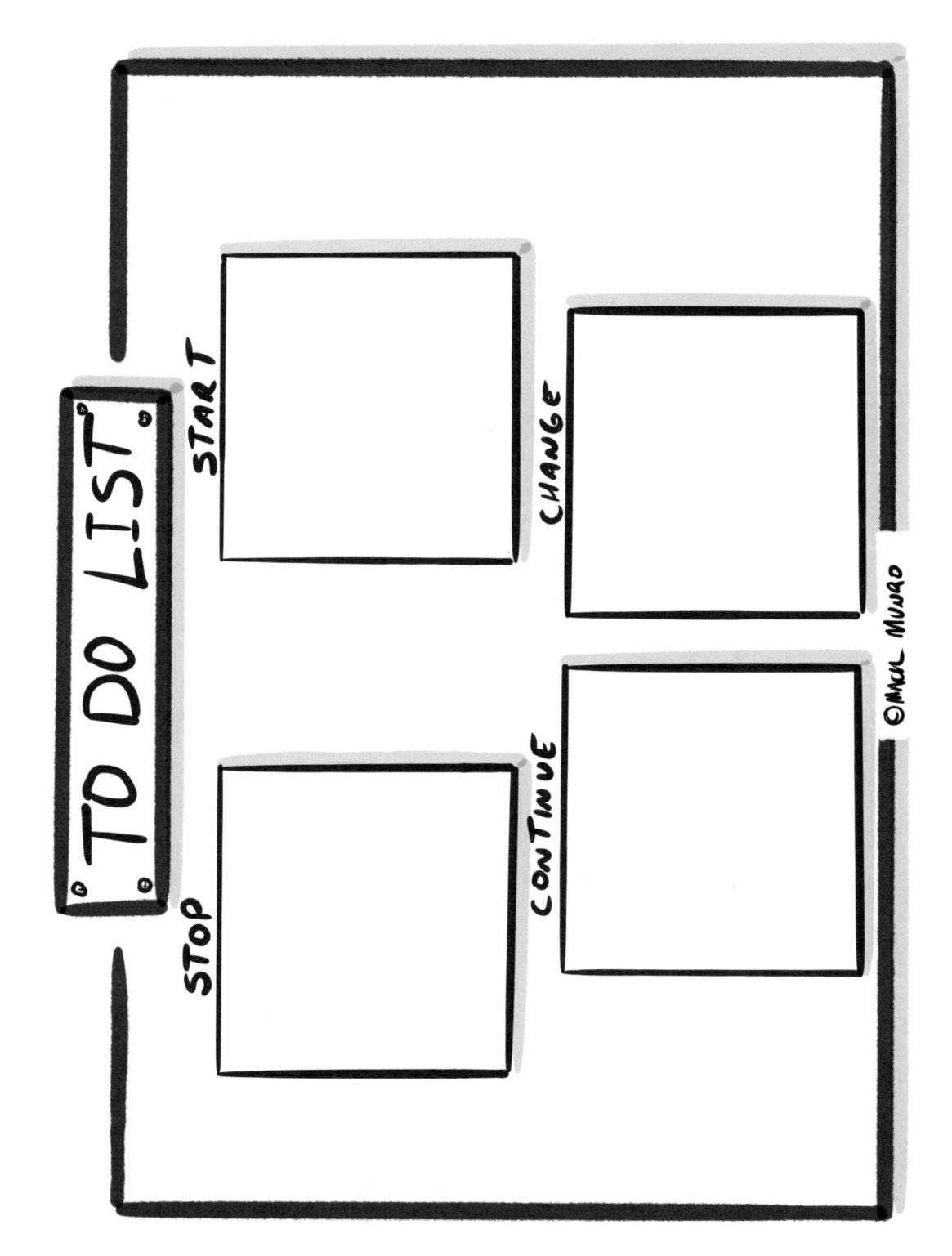

START

CHANGE

STOP

CONTINUE

© Neal Munro

116 | THE ART OF BEING A GREAT BOSS

Worksheet: Dealing with a Poor Performer

1. **Specific Issue to Address:**

2(a). **Current Standard for that Task/Job**

2(b). **Employee's Current Result for that Task/Job**

3. *S: (SUBJECTIVE):* *(What you hear anecdotally)*

   O: (OBJECTIVE): *(What you observe. Hard data)*

4. **Have the Conversation**

   S:

   W:

   E:

   A:

   R:

5. **Follow up on:** _____

Worksheet: Development Conversations

1. Specific Issue to Address:

2(a). Current Standard for that Task/Job

2(b). Employee's Current Result for that Task/Job

3. Which Development Phase are they in?

4. What's the Issue? (Skill/Will/Focus)

5. Pick your strategy:

A Medical Device That Saves a Career

Harvey Hatfield has been a Product Development Director for BLACK STAR Medical Devices for about four years. In this post, he is responsible for the development of new products at the 50-plus-years-old medical device company.

Two factors drive the product development process at BLACK STAR: 1) the rapid advances in medicine, and 2) the cyclical market (70% of sales coming after the first of the year). Product Development Teams must be able to conceive, design, and produce their product quickly to capitalize on the current market trends and ensure marketing, product recognition, and availability during the marketing period. All new product prototypes must be reviewed, approved, and funded by the Product Committee, composed of the CEO, VP of Finance, and VP of Marketing.

Harvey's team has recently completed the development and initial testing of what he believes will be a major new device, SNOREAWAY. The brainchild of one of the departments' best minds, SNOREAWAY represents a new generation of sleep apnea devices that are designed to be used interactively with specific types of music and link exclusively with online music services such as *Spotify* and *Pandora*. Harvey expects that SNOREAWAY and its support pieces will have major market impact if introduced in late September. It could mean significant revenues for BLACK STAR. It is important to Harvey personally, as well as for BLACK STAR, to have a successful season. Sales have been down for the past two years and Research and Development is under pressure to better its performance. Last year's major product line, COLO-ROOTER (a pre-colonoscopy cleansing tool), was introduced late because of design improvements requested by Quality Testing and subsequent necessary machinery modifications. As a result, it did not perform up to expectations. If this year's product line is not successful, Harvey anticipates a reduction in funding for the department and the possibility of some or all of his function being outsourced.

Preliminary market analysis indicates that SNOREAWAY could be a crossover device, appealing to not only humans, but also animals who tend to snore loudly, keeping their owners awake. The potential is enormous. However, to make it successful, Harvey is going to need a significant increase in immediate funding for testing and startup costs, as well as the guarantee of available funding for an extensive marketing effort to kick off and establish the product. Being part of a new generation of devices, SNOREAWAY has the potential to become synonymous with the field if the right foundation is built. In short, to do it right will require a large commitment of capital, but Harvey believes that BLACK STAR's future depends on it. Harvey and his design team have decided to develop a plan for ensuring that SNOREAWAY gets approved by the Product Committee and receives the financing that it needs to succeed. They review what they know about the players:

George Smith —CEO and chairman of the Product Committee. George rose up through the ranks at BLACK STAR over a period of 28 years. He has been CEO for the past five years. Because of two years of flat profits, George has been under increasing pressure from the board to enhance the company's performance. While heading the Product Committee, George has always supported team decision-making for new products, believing in the committee's collective wisdom. He trusts the people who report to him and offers them loyalty in return. While Harvey has not spoken directly to George about SNOREAWAY (in fact, Harvey hasn't had much contact with George at all), he believes that the CEO may have concerns about the initial startup costs for Production and Marketing, and that he might see the new product as too risky.

Russell Jones —Director of Quality Testing. Russell reports directly to George Smith. Harvey sees Russell as his biggest roadblock to gaining approval. As Director of Quality Testing, Russell was directly responsible for the delay in introducing last year's new product COLO-ROOTER (his exact comment was *"how in the world are we going to market something that people stick up their rear end?"*). He is, by training, an engineer, and is relatively new to BLACK STAR, having come on board four years earlier to head the newly formed "testing" function. Because quality is so important at BLACK STAR, testing was placed directly under the CEO in the table of organization. Russell has a good relationship with George, who values his opinion. That is of concern to Harvey because he knows that Russell will be leery of any new technology, and especially so of this proposal since it comes from Harvey's group. Harvey and Russell never did hit it off, and since Russell's delay of the COLO-ROOTER product-line, there has been bad blood between them. They simply do not trust one another. Russell has been a proponent of outsourcing the R&D function. In fact, this year he has gone so far as to approach the Product Committee with a product proposal—NASALREAMER, a seasonal allergy remedy, generated by an outside design-source.

Susan Oliver —VP of Marketing. A member of the Product Committee, Susan is bright, ambitious, and looking to position herself to take over for the CEO when he retires. The smart money says that will be within the next two years. But Susan needs to demonstrate to the Board that she can envision BLACK STAR's needs and make the right decisions for the company. Her support of last year's "big product bust," COLO-ROOTER, cast doubt on her decision making in the eyes of some board members. She has a very good relationship with George Smith and she absolutely detests Russell Jones for his role in delaying the COLO-ROOTER *("Who is Russell to tell me I can't sell something? I'll demo COLO-ROOTER on him right now!")* product last year. Since marketing is such a critical part of any product's potential success, Susan is seen as being a key decision maker at BLACK STAR. Harvey is somewhat concerned about Susan. He was the one who pitched COLO-ROOTER to her, and since its failure, their relationship has been cooler than he would like it. While Susan has not openly opposed SNOREAWAY, she appears concerned about the potential retooling costs.

Ed Harris —Director of Marketing. Ed reports directly to Susan Oliver. Susan relies a great deal on Ed, who is her heir apparent. He is a great source of information about all things marketing. While not a member of the Product Committee, Ed's opinion does matter. Susan respects his judgment and business acumen. Harvey and Ed have a good relationship. Ed has expressed guarded interest in the SNOREAWAY product line and, while not a direct supporter, sees it as having considerable potential.

Gloria Rawlings —VP of Finance and member of the Product Committee. Gloria is seen as relatively neutral at this point. She has a good relationship with the CEO and other members of the committee. Although Harvey hasn't had much contact with her, he has heard through the grapevine that she is very cautious and likely to consider the product too risky. Harvey has heard through a personal friend that Gloria has been quietly speaking with the Board of another corporation about leaving BLACK STAR to take a new position as their CFO. Harvey believes that if this were to become public knowledge, BLACK STAR's CEO would view Gloria as disloyal and possibly remove her from her position.

Mark Levinson —Director of Operations. Mark reports directly to George Smith. Mark essentially serves as the plant manager for BLACK STAR's production facilities. He has been with the company for more than 20 years and has spoken of retiring in the next 3–4 years. Mark is a no-nonsense, hands-on engineer who sees his role as holding the organization together. He would very much like to see BLACK STAR positioned well for the future. When Harvey has spoken with him about SNOREAWAY, he has been enthusiastic about its potential. In fact, he has been working on some ideas that he believes will reduce the retooling costs for SNOREAWAY. Mark has a good relationship with Harvey and the CEO.

1. What is Harvey's biggest challenge right now? What is the ROOT CAUSE of this problem?

2. What specific actions should Harvey take to achieve his goal in this situation?

3. Will your suggestion work? If not, how can you prepare to head off obstacles?

About Your Instructor

Mack Munro is Founder and CEO of **Boss Builders** and an experienced author, speaker, and consultant. He is the author of ***How to Be a Great Boss*** and 5 other business books.

Boss Builders has provided management training to corporations of all sizes and in nearly every industry both in the United States and abroad.

Boss Builders

P.O. Box 75
Vanleer, TN 37181
(931) 221-2988

Made in the USA
Columbia, SC
01 February 2025